Abuses

Abuses

Alphonso Lingis

✳✳✳✳✳✳✳✳✳✳✳✳✳✳

UNIVERSITY OF CALIFORNIA PRESS
Berkeley / Los Angeles / London

University of California Press
Berkeley and Los Angeles, California

University of California Press
London, England

Library of Congress Cataloging-in-Publication Data
Lingis, Alphonso, 1933–
    Abuses / Alphonso Lingis.
      p.   cm.
    Includes bibliographical references.
    ISBN 0-520-08631-7 (alk. paper)
    1. Lingis, Alphonso, 1933–   —Journeys.   2. Voyages and travels.
I.   Title.
G465.L56   1994
910.4—dc20   93-40254
                                                                        CIP

Printed in the United States of America

1   2   3   4   5   6   7   8   9

Truth font designed by Barry Deck © 1993
All photographs are by the author.

Contents

These were letters written to friends, from places I found myself for months at a time, about encounters that moved me and troubled me. Letters from Mexico, Cuba, Peru, the Philippines, Nicaragua, Antarctica, Brazil, France, Thailand, India, Bali, Bangladesh, Guatemala.

The letters were almost never answered, maybe never read. Nowadays people only write letters to record requests, transactions, and detailed explanations, or to send brief greetings; when they want to make personal contact, they telephone. Conversation by telephone communicates with the tone and warmth of the human voice, but what moved one deeply can only be shared through language when one has found the right words. Finding the right words takes time, and the one to whom they are addressed is no longer the one you thought he or she was when you wrote. One sends one's letters to an address he or she has left.

It is hard to share something only with words on a silent page. As the places and encounters reverberated in my heart, I found again and again they had not been said with the right words. What I wrote about them finally became too long to send to anyone. I will again find they have not been said with the right words.

To whom, gathered together in this book, are these pages now being addressed? To friends whose names and addresses I do not know. To you, in Mexico, Cuba, Peru, the Philippines, Nicaragua, Antarctica, Brazil, France, Thailand, India, Bali, Bangladesh, Guatemala, and in places I have never or not yet visited, you who are moved and troubled by what and by whom you encounter there.

It is you who teach me the right words. To find the right words is not only to find the words that convey the tone, the pacing, and the progression of the event; it is also to find the words that communicate to others because they are the words and forms of speech of those others. And though I do not know your names or addresses, these writings have no other purpose than to learn one day from your words the events and encounters that have moved and troubled you. I do call you friends, because it has long seemed to me that a friendship where one does not teach one another becomes shallow and meaningless. Everyone who, while wandering along the shore of whatever continent or island, has found a letter put in a bottle and cast into the sea, has found a friend.

These writings also became no longer my letters. I found myself only trying to speak for others, others greeted only with passionate kisses of parting.

What I wrote was how places and events spoke to me. What persons my nation and my culture have made enemies said to me. What people my nation and my culture have conquered and silenced said to me with their mute bodies. What in sordid places their bodies beautiful and sublime beyond beautiful said to me. What their animal passions said to me. What persons who were dying and had nothing to say about the unknowable they were not advancing but drifting toward said to me by the endurance with which they bore this last journey. What ruined temples and departed gods said to me. I understood that what they said to me they were saying to you.

When the other is there and able to speak himself or herself, he or she listens to the thoughts one formulates for him or her, and assents to them or contests them or withdraws from them into the silence from which he or she came. One only speaks for others when they are silent or silenced. And to speak for others is to silence oneself.

One will say that the philosophical reflections I elaborated were my own. Did not Nietzsche say that philosophy is the most spiritual form of the will to power? It is true that I studied philosophy books, and teach them. Philosophy is abstract and universal speech. It is speech that is not clothed, armed, invested with the authority of a particular god, ancestor, or institution, speech that does not program operations and produce results, speech barren and destitute. It is speech that is destined for all, speech that subjects whatever it says to the contestation of anyone from any culture or history or latitude, accepts any stranger as its judge.

Then what is distinctive about philosophy is not a certain vocabulary and grammar of dead metaphors and empirically unverifiable generalizations. One's own words become philosophy, and not the operative paradigms of a culture of which one is a practitioner, in the measure that the voices of those silenced by one's culture and its practices are heard in them.

I

*****

Tenochtitlán

There were no cars parked in the streets, and no one
walking. There were no shops, no sidewalk stalls of
newspapers or soft drinks. I inquired several times
from the armed police at corners to find the street.
Rows of trees stretched over ten-foot-high stone walls
with two or three electronically operated doors cut in
them on each block. When I found the number, I
pushed the buzzer and identified myself on the inter-
com. The lawyer himself opened the door for me. Our
mutual acquaintance in the States he had known for
years; they had first met, he said, on the beach, at
Cancun. He invited me to pull my car inside his compound. "A hundred cars a day are stolen in this city,"
he said with a smile, "and yours is new and beautiful." He led me into his marble-floored home, introduced me to his wife, also a lawyer. We sat in the
salon; a maid put margaritas and hors d'oeuvres on
the onyx table before us. When he built this house,
the lawyer recalled, Tlalpan was a village on the
south of the city, blessed with its clean air at the base
of the Ajusco volcano. Already at the beginning of the
colonial period, the viceroys built subsidiary resi-
dences here. Now many movie actors and actresses
live in Tlalpan, in palaces I did not see behind those
walls. There is also a medical center reserved for senior government officials; it is decorated, the lawyer's
wife said, with frescos by Siqueiros, Chavez Morado,
and Nishizawa. The lawyer and his wife had both

decided to retire two years ago. Since then, they traveled, to the States, then to France, Spain, and Italy,
after that to Japan, Singapore, and Hong Kong, most
recently to Australia. They had visited our mutual
acquaintance in Philadelphia, and he had come to
visit them, stayed with them in Cancun and in Acapulco. The lawyer's wife asked me about Kathmandu;
I also described Bali and Bangkok. We had another
margarita and then another. We got up to go contemplate an African mask over the fireplace, a tenth-
century Khmer Buddha in the hall, an Australian
boomerang. We went at random from one continent
to another, savoring the names of new places to go to.

In Honduras they are filling cargo ships with pine-
apples, coffee, and tobacco for us; at the port of Balik-
papan in Kalimantan they are filling the oil tankers
that will fuel the cargo ships; in the dunes of Mo-
rocco they are shoveling phosphates; on the beaches
of Malaysia they are scooping up tin; in Zimbabwe
they are digging in pits for the diamonds; in Zaire
they are mining uranium. But we don't just stay
home and wait for the doorbell to ring. We ourselves
go there, to them. We go to Acapulco, to Jamaica, to
La Paz, to Tangier, to Fiji, to Pattaya. We find ourselves welcome; jet package tours are one of the most
important developments in the economies of former
colonies in those continents since our last world war.
In some of the smaller of these new nations the majority of the resident population consists of busboys,
waitresses, gardeners, tour-bus drivers. Certainly we
do not go to Acapulco to look into our investments
there; one is on vacation. One does not go to poke
around in the hamlets of a backwater of the civil-
ized world; one stays in a Hyatt or an Intercontinental. We would not go there to find something for

ourselves in the Aztec civilization swept into dust 450
years ago. One goes to the Anthropological Museum
in downtown Mexico City. Or one did, until two years
ago when the key pieces were dispersed in an un-
solved robbery. In the past twenty years, enterprising
bands of men have located most of the Maya sites in
what is left of the Yucatán rain forests, dislodged
their notable carvings with crow bars, and cut them
with power saws into pieces of the size to decorate
our living rooms. The pieces are to be seen in Austin,
Nice, Kuwait. In Acapulco one bronzes one's skin, one
swims, water-skis, goes parasailing, scuba diving, and
shopping. One encounters the locals, the best-looking
young creoles and mestizos and Indians, groomed,
liveried, who bring cocktails and cocaine and themselves. In Pattaya the tourist season coincides with the
dry season; for five month there is a resident population of fifty-five thousand prostitutes. But prostitute is
too harsh and misleading a term for those upcountry
adolescents who are the sole subsistence for whole
families during the five-month drought. The airline
hostesses are the geisha girls of these decades, and it
is their affability, their availability, their graces, and
their slang the country girls try to learn and imitate
in their untrained and touching ways.

On the planes, we ship them back ourselves. They
bought us, with all their bananas and uranium and
diamonds. But we are not another commodity in the
global economy. What after all can they do with us,
but garland, feed, and massage us? The term prostitute decidedly belongs to an obsolete vocabulary. We
have not sold them ourselves for money. For we have
become values. That is, money.

The heat of the afternoon passed. The driver
pulled out the lawyer's car; we drove through San

Angel where through wrought-iron spiked gates we
caught glimpses into colonial gardens. We got out of
the car at Coyoacán to visit the remaining outbuild-
ing of Cortés's palace. On the site of the palace itself,
a Dominican church had been built; the lawyer and
his wife had been married there. Inside, benediction
was concluding; we knelt as the priest swung the
monstrance, a four-foot-wide gold sun, over us, *Domi-
nus vobiscum*. We walked over to see a building said
to be the palace of la Malinche, the Aztec girl who
had traded her nation for Cortés's affections, and the
house where Leon Trotsky was assassinated.

We returned to Tlalpan; we drove through the
gates of a wall that extended across the whole block:
this had been the home of a surgeon the lawyer had
known since childhood, and who had lived here with
his wife and one son. The building extended the full
length of the block-long back wall; before it were
gardens with sleeping swans and peafowl. The owners
had sold the mansion with all its furnishings to a
restauranteur and had moved to the Costa del Sol in
Spain. Inside, the walls were decorated with huge
portraits of racehorses. We ordered margaritas and
hors d'oeuvres; the waiter brought three silver dishes
with oily inch-long eel fry, white termites' eggs, and
gusanos de maguey, finger-size segmented worms that
are found in the maguey plants from whose white
milk-sap the Aztecs derived, and today the campesinos
derive, a fermented drink called *pulque*. The waiter
showed me how to fold the wiry little eels into a tor-
tilla with guacamole and piquant sauce. Then we had
steak, cut, the waiter assured us, from bulls killed in
the corrida the day before.

The lawyer refused me the honor of paying the
bill. They would write our mutual acquaintance in

Philadelphia what a gift he had sent them in the pleasure of my company—how much I knew, how much I had seen. Back at the compound, the driver parked the lawyer's car and I unlocked mine. We embraced; how easily we had come to know and love one another! The lawyer went inside and returned to give me a blade of carved obsidian, which as a boy he had found in the rubble and weeds at Teotihuacán and which an archeologist had dated for him as belonging to the second half of the first century B.C. The Aztecs believed that the pyramid of the sun at Teotihuacán was built by the vanished Toltecs at the beginning of their cosmic era, that of the Fifth Sun, which Aztec astrologers and priests had predicted was to come to an end in the year *Nahui ollin.* It was in the year Nahui ollin that Hernando Cortés landed on the beach of Chalchuihcuecán, which he renamed Vera Cruz.

Between 1521 and 1536 Spanish conquistadors and missionaries put an end to all the great civilizations of America—Aztec, Mixtec, Zapotec, Pipil, and Inca. Of their cities, their social order, their science, their gods, wrote Bernal Díaz del Castillo in his *True History of the Conquest of New Spain,* "all . . . is overthrown and lost, nothing left standing."[1] Pope Alexander VI, who had granted to the Catholic monarchs of Spain and Portugal the lands of all the heathens of the world, issued bulls granting plenary indulgences in advance for all sins committed in the Conquest. The superiority of the new Christian dispensation did not lie in its horror of war and human sacrifice; the conquistadors conquered because their wars were more treacherous and their massacres more wanton. The superiority lay in that the Christian conquistadors brought love to the worshippers of Quetzalcoatl.

That is, money. Although Tenochtitlán, built in
the crater lake of an enormous dead volcano, was an
immense market, the Aztecs, the Egret People, did
not know money. The wealth arrived as tributes and
gifts, and was distributed by prestations and barter.
Gold was used to plate the walls of temples; there
were no gold coins in Tenochtitlán.

Tributes made, gifts given, impose claims on the
receiver. A regime of gifts is a regime of debts. Marcel Mauss, in his work *The Gift* (1923),[2] showed that
it is an economic system; indeed, it is the most exact-
ing economic order. It is an economy of rigorous
reciprocity; each gift proffered requires the return of
the equivalent. In the economy of gifts man became
man, that is, Nietzsche wrote, the evaluator.[3] The
herd animal learned to reckon, to appraise, to calculate, to remember; he became rational. He learned his
own worth. The self-domesticated animal, a productive organism with use value, became an exchange
value.

Money introduces a factor of nonreciprocity. One
receives something useful, and one renders in return
artifacts without utilizable properties. There is immediate discharge of indebtedness. One arises as a person, free to choose and to give—a value unto oneself. "Working against the narrow and rigorous moral
discriminations of Subsistence economies—where
love cannot be developed as a value in itself though
its semblances are enforced—money vitiates strict
reciprocities and differentiates given roles and stat-
uses so as to provide options impossible in situations
where *giving* = *receiving*," Kenelm Burridge writes.
"Handling money, thinking about and 'being thought'
and constrained by it, vitiates firm dyadic relationships and makes possible the perception of oneself as

a unitary being ranged against other unitary beings.
The opportunity is presented to become and to be
singular."[4]

When Hernando Cortés forced Moctezoma Xocoyotzin to take him to the summit of the Uitzilopochtli
pyramid, the charnel-house stench of the blood-soaked
priests of the war god filled him with revulsion. He
prevailed upon Moctezoma to erect on the same summits as these demons images of Jesus Universal Re-
deemer and of the Virgin Mother. Yet the knights of
Cortés certainly made no objection to the slaughter of
captives and noncombatants, nor did their priests, who
established the Inquisition in Mexico six years after
the fall of Tenochtitlán. The Mesoamericanists today
calculate the population of Mexico upon the arrival of
Cortés variously between nine and twenty-five million; but they agree that it was reduced to one million during the first fifty years of the Conquest.

The Aztec civilization is singled out in revulsion
for having made of human sacrifice a religious ritual.
Bernal Díaz identifies Uitzilopochtli, "The Hummingbird of the Left," with Satan, since, without promise
of any afterlife, the supreme religious act of his worshippers is the shedding of human blood. Only brave
soldiers killed in battle or sacrificed were promised a
return, to the earth as hummingbirds, whose plumage
was woven into the shimmering raiment of the pre-
siding Aztec officials. Bernal Díaz recognized here a
religion of the most perverted form, utterly alien to
any gospel, any kind of salvation.

Yet the conquistadors were not liberal Protestants
assembling on Sundays for the purpose of listening to
a moral exhortation; Catholic Christianity is a religion
centered on sacrifice. The redemption brought to an
earth damned since Adam's sin was wrought by deity

becoming human in order to be led to sacrifice. Each
Sunday the Catholic community assembles before an
altar in which that sacrifice is, not commemorated,
but really reenacted. If each Christian is not enjoined
actually to carry a cross to a gibbet in his turn, that is
not because the sacrifice of the Son of Man freed
mankind from any destination to be sacrificed; it is
that he must not add his ransom to that of Jesus who
gave his life for all men. But the Christian life can
only consist in a real participation in the redemptive
act of the Christ. To be a Christian is to make each
moment, each act, each thought, each perception of
one's existence a sacrifice. Not simply in partial and
intermittent acts of mortification, which would com-
pensate for acts of indulgence, but in a total putting
to death of the flesh and of the world. "With Christ I
am nailed to the cross. It is now no longer I that live,
but Christ lives in me" (Gal 2:19).

The Aztec religion did not require quantitatively
more human sacrifice than did the Christian. It was
the purpose of sacrifice that differed. Jesus died for
our redemption. In the Eden God created, nothing
was wanting in the waters above and the waters below, in the skies and on the dry land; the only vice
was man—more exactly, woman. Humankind corrupted itself, and against it several times the waters
rose again over the dry land in a decreation, from
which, for the sake of Noah, of Jonah, of ten just
men in Ninevah, of Abraham, a remnant was spared.
Paul recognized in Jesus a new Adam; the old mankind must now perish entirely. "For we know that
our old self has been crucified with him, in order that
the body of sin may be destroyed, that we may no
longer be slaves to sin; for he who is dead is acquitted
of sin" (Rom 6:6–7). The remnant saved by Jesus is

not cleansed but reborn, in the waters from which all skies, dry land, fishes and flying things, creeping and crawling things once came. The new life is destined, not for this now corrupted world, but for the new Eden, and for immortality. Through mortification of his whole nature, the Christian accedes to definitive deathlessness.

On the pyramids of Tenochtitlán, sacrifice had nothing to do with human salvation, nor with attainment of deathlessness through death. The Aztec religion was a religion not of eternity but of time. All the deities were units of time. Each day had its deity, each day was a deity, a deity was a day. If the Aztec astronomers climbed the summits of pyramids by night to chart the stars and record the comets and labored by day to calculate the periodicity of eclipses and meteors on the orbits of cosmic time, this astronomy and this mathematics were not of religious application; it was theology and of the most pressing cosmic urgency. For as each god has its day, each polyhedron of deities and each table has its time. Every fifty-two years all the orbits reach an equilibrium; the Aztecs could find nothing in all their nocturnal searching of the immense stretches of nothingness between the stars that would guarantee that this stasis could not continue indefinitely, and all motion, all life come to an end. It would then be necessary that motion be liberated, that it not be contained within the beings that move themselves. The Aztecs poured forth their blood in order to give to the most remote astral deities, suspended for a night in the voids, movement.

At the great ceremony of Cuahuitlehua, the children of the Egret People born within the past year were taken to the temple of Tlaloc, where the priests drew blood from the earlobes of the infant girls and from the genitals of the infant boys. Adults regularly drew blood from their earlobes, tongues, thighs, upper arms, chests, or genitals. Each day in the palaces the nobles pierced their ears, their nipples, their penises and testicles with maguey thorns in order that blood flow to the heavens. The Aztec imperial order did not, like a Roman empire, extend its administration ever further over subject societies and economies; it existed to drain ever greater multitudes of blood-sacrifices toward the pyramids of the sun the Aztecs erected upon the earth, that monster whose maw swallows the setting sun, the remains of the dead, and sacrificial victims. A youth destined to have no children, the sacrificial victim, arrayed as a god Tezcatli-poca, "The Mirror's Smoke," ascended the pyramid to the heavens: he was man set forth as the absolute value, absolute as that which does not exchange what belongs to him for anything he or his kin could receive in return. Theologian Bartolomé de las Casas wrote: "The Nations that offered human sacrifice to their gods, misled idolaters that they were, showed the lofty idea that they had of the excellence of divinity, the value of their gods, and how noble, how exalted was their veneration of divinity. They consequently demonstrated that they possessed, better than other nations, natural reflection, uprightness of speech and judgment of reason; better than others they used their understanding. And in religiousness they surpassed all other nations, for the most religious nations of the world are those that offer in sacrifice their own children."[5]

The conquistadors and the monks brought love to the Mexica. The Aztecs, Bernal Díaz reports dismally, were sodomites, as were the Mayas of Cape Catoche,

the Cempoalans, the Xocotlans, the Tlascalans. Sodomist was their religion: In the first Indian prayer
house he and his companions came upon on the Mexican coast, Bernal Díaz reports finding idols of baked
clay, very ugly, which represented Indians sodomizing
one another. Of the Indians of whom the conquistadors had any knowledge, the exception was Moctezoma II himself, despite his gastronomic taste for the
flesh of young boys. It was this, rather than his elegant manners and his gullibility, that commanded the
respect of the conquistadors. Cortés assigned a Spanish
page to him to test him, and found him incorruptible.
When, during the final battle, they turned on him
with daggers, Moctezoma requested Catholic baptism.
The priest, occupied in breaking through the walls of
the palace in search of the treasure, did not come;
Moctezoma died without the Catholic redemption.
Today he is worshipped as a god in San Cristóbal and
Cuaxtla.

The sodomy Bernal Díaz perceived is not contemporary homosexuality, nor that of Greek classicism
and Renaissance humanism. Sodomy, determined in
the juridic discourse, civic and canonical, of Christendom, is conceptualized not as a nature but as an act, a
transgression of divine, human, and natural positive
law. Not simply unnatural, according to the ideology
of perversion and degeneration of the modern period,
which explained it positively by a fault in nature,
explained it thereby by nature—sodomy is antinatu-
ral. It issues not from an unconscious compulsion but
from an intellect that conceives the law and a will
that determines to defy it; it derives from libertinage
and not from sensuality. Sodomy is the use of the
erected male organ not to direct the germ for the
propagation of the species nor to give pleasure to the

partner but to gore the partner and release the germ
of the race in its excrement. It attacks the human
species as such. Not only does it invert the natural
finality of organs by which we came to exist; it is
directed against the imperative to maintain the genus
which every positive law, every universal, must pre-
suppose. It is the last limit of outrage under the eyes
of the monotheist god, God the Father, that unengen-
dered principle of all generation and absolutized formula for the normative. It is the act that isolates, that
singularizes absolutely. Positively, sodomy is the crime
in which sovereignty is constituted and resides. It is
the act, unmotivated and unjustifiable, that posits the
singular one, the monster. This singular, singularizing
act can only be incessantly repeated, rending the
monotheist time of universal generation, conjuring up
a cosmic theater without order or sanction in which
trajectories of time rush to their dissipation.

When Cortés burnt his ships before advancing
upon Tenochtitlán, when they were but four hundred
slashing their way through the enraged Aztec citadel,
what maintained the epic resolve in the conquistadors
was their horror at falling into the hands of these
sodomites and being sacrificed on the altars of their
demons thirsty for the blood of the human species. "It
must seem very strange to my readers," Bernal Díaz
writes, "that I should have suffered from this unac-
customed terror. For I had taken part in many battles,
from the time when I made the voyage of discovery
with Francisco Hernandez de Cordoba till the defeat
of our army on the causeway under Alvarado. But up
to that time when I saw the cruel deaths inflicted on
our comrades before our very eyes, I had never felt
such fear as I did in these last battles." "I must say
that when I saw my comrades dragged up each day to

the altar, and their chests struck open and their palpi-
tating hearts drawn out, and when I saw the arms
and legs of these sixty-two men cut off and eaten, I
feared that one day or another they would do the
same to me."[6] Certainly it was not the painfulness of
the Aztec sacrifice as compared to the burning under
slow fires that Cortés preferred (and which the Inquisition sanctioned, since this method of execution does
not produce the shedding of blood, which would risk
making the death of heretics an image of the shedding of the redemptive blood of Jesus) that so horri-
fied conquistador Bernal Díaz; it was the monstrous
and sodomist cause for which there was sacrifice.

Bernal Díaz knew that the Aztec priests daily let
their own blood flow forth to their gods, and that the
sacrificial victims, drawn from courts everywhere in
the Aztec empire, and whom he perceived, through
empirical induction from the idols he had seen at
every stage of the advance toward Tenochtitlán rather
than through knowledge of Aztec sexual legislation, to
be sodomites, were treated as incarnations of the gods
and climbed willingly the calvary of the Aztec pyramids. If Quauhtemotzin destined Cortés for sacrifice
on the altar of Uitzilopochtli, The Hummingbird of
the Left, it is because he perceived him as Quetzalcoatl. What then would be a sodomite who sacrificed
himself?

Aztec sacrifice was not at all for our salvation, for
the salvation of the Mexica, the people of Anahuac,
"The One World," or of the human species. Its purpose was cosmic and not anthropocentric; with the
volcanic obsidian dagger the human blood is released
for the sake of the cosmic order or, more exactly, in
order that the diurnal gods rise and fall, that the divine trajectories of time rush to their extinction. The

blood that makes our bodies move themselves is released from them in order that time and not the
stasis of eternity be. The apparition of the human
species and the reproduction of a human politico-
economic order are not guaranteed by a cosmic order, but are sacrificed to move the cosmic trajectories
to their expiration. This religion assigns to man the
most exorbitant destiny ever conceived in any system
of thought.

The destiny their religion assigned to the Egret
People requires an existence that has broken with
that of homo politicus, homo oeconomicus, an existence no longer a subject of, and a value in, reproduction and production. Such a human existence is
no longer commanded by a nature that maintains
itself—no longer commanded by universals without (incarnated in the individual in the form of
the instinct to reproduce the species) nor by self-
regenerating compulsions of one's own sensuous
nature. The Aztec sacrificial offering is an existence
that realizes absolute singularity.

In Christendom sacrifice is required by original
sin. The concept of a sin of which all humans are
guilty because all are Adam's children is not really
the epistemological short circuit produced where the
juridic concept of guilt was wired into the biological
idea of heredity. Sin is not the ethical-juridic concept of guilt which is elaborated in the theory of vol-
untariness in Aristotle's *Nicomachean Ethics*. Ethical
culpability is imputed to the will and is coextensive
with consciousness. One's sin exceeds the measure
of consciousness, as all the anguish of Job argues,
and the sinner must first pray to know his sin. The
notion of sin, depicted as exile, retains what was essential in the archaic notion of stain: evil as a state.

The movement in the act that puts one in the state of
sin is not the transgression as such, transgression of a
positive law of the order in which one has been do-
mesticated; in the sinful act there is a turning away,
an existential conversion from God out of which all
transgressions issue.

The concept of original sin identifies the origin of
this deviation not in the conscious choice of the individual but in the individual as participant in the history of a people. Saint Augustine of Hippo saw that
the tale told in Genesis does not isolate an individual
faculty of choice but depicts a collusion of male and
female nature in the tasting of the fruit of the tree of
the knowledge of good and evil.

Born of flesh, the individual turns back to flesh
and to the state of sin that is in all flesh. Saint Paul,
in the Epistle to the Romans, had spoken of the inner
mystery of iniquity: "For I know that in me, that is,
in my flesh, no good dwells, because to wish is within
my power, but I do not find the strength to accom-
plish what is good. For I do not the good that I wish,
but the evil that I do not wish, that I perform" (Rom
7:18–20). The flesh, in Paul, is not a concept related
to the Aristotelian physics of the hylomorphic composition of human substance; it is the emblem of the
opacity of a will that does not effect itself.

In Eden, Saint Augustine explains, the will in
mind which views the goodness of creation directs the
sensuous will; orgasm occurs when the will in sensuous nature sinks into itself and the will in mind collapses. The supreme pleasure of orgasm is supreme
not simply in quantitative degree but in that it is
most fully one's own; one's will actively participates
in and wills this collapse of will. Orgasm is then not
just the exemplary, or the most compulsive instance

of the will not effecting itself; it is the realization of
sin as a state—original sin as originating sinfulness, a
state where the will does not perform the good because it wills its own nullity. The existential exile
involved in the originating sinfulness is a turning
toward nullity; it is also, for each one, his or her pri-
mary way of participating in the history of a people.
One's sinfulness is not a property, like racial color or
specific morphology, that would be transmitted in the
conjunction of sperm with ovum; it is an antiproperty,
it is the willed defection of will in which one is conceived and conceives.

In the time of Noah, of Jonah, of Abraham, the
Creator did not hesitate to engulf the material world
in order to put to death carnal humankind. The
Christ eternally engendered by the Creator became
incarnate, entered into this flesh of nullity, in order to
be sacrificed, and in order to put to death with his
death carnal concupiscent humanity. In Jesus the Creator of the material world is himself put to death in
order that his creation no longer conceive and reproduce in sin, in order that through the death of carnal
nature humankind accede to deathlessness.

The Christian lives in the image and likeness of
God, in the imitation of God; he and she procreate as
God creates, as the Virgin Mary conceived, without
the orgasmic delirium. The Christian reproduces human life in an act of making of his or her carnal nature a sacrificial offering.

Augustine's theology does not devalue man's carnal
nature but values it absolutely in the divine economy
of redemption. In the economy of sin, giving himself the
supreme pleasure of orgasm, man ever augments his
debt, which cannot be paid out of the nothingness of
will concupiscence engenders. In the sublime economy

of redemption, the substance whose use value is null, the carnal nature willing its own nullity of will, becomes the measure of the exchange value of all goods of use value. The value of concupiscence is no longer measured by the new, but equally concupiscent life it produces. The value of our carnal substance is measured by the infinite value of the flesh of God sacrificed to redeem it and by the infinite series of earthly goods to be sacrificed for its unending mortification. It is the money of the city of God.

There is an inner economy in the man who participates in political economy, in the City of Man and in the City of God. It is by reason of his organism that man is homo oeconomicus. It is also by reason of the economy of the polis that the infant becomes an organism.

An infant is tubes disconnected, corpuscle full of yolk put out of the fluid reservoir of the womb, gasping, gulping free air, pumping, circulating fluids. The disconnected tubes are open to multiple couplings, multiple usages. A mouth is a coupling that draws in fluid, but can also slobber or vomit it out forcibly; that babbles or cries, can pout, smile, spit, and kiss. From the first the mouth that draws in sustenance also produces an excess, foam, slaver, extends a surface of warm pleasure, an erotogenic surface in contact with the surface of the maternal breast. The coupling is not only consuming, of sustenance, but productive, of pleasure, spread, shared. The anus is an orifice that ejects the segments of flow, but also holds them in, ejects vapors, noise, can pout, be coaxed, refuses, defiles, and defies. And spreads its excesses, producing a warm and viscous surface and surface effects of pleasure. The excrement is waste and gratuity; it is the archetypal gift, which is a transfer without recompense, not of one's possessions, one's things, but of oneself.

In time, the hand couples onto the penis, finds the surfaces of contact productive of viscous warmth, spreading a surface of pleasure. The child discovers the pleasures of wasting his seed; he smears around this liquid currency, he produces a surface of waste again, and surface effects of pleasure. He adheres to this viscous pleasure, wills this waste, this nullity; this will actively participates in and wills this collapse of domestic will. He would like to seduce the mother into this potlatch economy.

These developments are being watched. The other intervenes, the father. The father claims proprietary rights over the mother, interdicts masturbation. The paternal word is not indicative, informative, but imperative; it is prohibition, it is law. The son is sentenced to castrate himself, that is, excise his penis as an organ for the production of pleasure, take it definitively out of anyone's reach.

The father had renounced his own presence as an erotogenic surface laid out before the infantile contact, in order to figure before the child with the force of his word, as law. The word of the father becomes incarnate in the son in order to castrate the penis through which the infantile substance is squandered so as to put this production of nullity, this collapse of domestic will, to death. He puts it to death with his own death, with the excoriation of his own flesh craving for erotogenic contact with his son. The father became incarnate in the son in order to be sacrificed and in order to put infancy to death with his death.

The child laughs at the paternal threat, empirically most frequently formulated in the name of the

father by the mother, even as she fondles him. He
will take the paternal word seriously the day he discovers the castration of the mother. In horror he
learns that the mother has already been mutilated.
The law is sanguinary.

At the same time he comes to realize the chance
he is. He comes to understand that he has been
pulled forth from that gaping wound between her
thighs; he comes to understand that he is the organ
of which she has been castrated. He comes to understand why all this time she has been holding him
close to herself, fondling him, drooling over him.
He recognizes reflected in her eyes something he
has not touched nor felt touched by her: the phallus,
absent organ severed from her, separated from him,
not even an image he sees in her eyes, only a floating mirage before them or a sign sought out by
them. He formulates the project of making himself
be that phallus of which his mother has been mutilated, in order to hold on himself her narcissist love.
He sets out to identify himself wholly with this phallic phantasm. He understands that her solicitude for
his needs reduces him to servility and parasitism; he
understands that she satisfies his needs in order to
frustrate the demand for gratuitous devotion, love,
his infancy put on her. He will exchange all his infantile needs for the phallic contours, phenomenal
form of void, he parades before her as an insatiable
sign, appeal and demand. It is this total investment
of himself in the phallus that makes it possible for
him to effect the castration of a part, his penis as
immediate pleasure-object, the paternal word demanded, as well as the polymorphously perverse erotogenic surface production about it. The phallus is
the phantasmal substance, of no use value for the

production of erotogenic pleasure, for which all carnal surfaces utilizable for the production of pleasure are exchanged—the carnal form of money.

In internalizing the paternal law as the law of his inner libidinal economy, in engendering a superego, the son puts himself in the place of the father. When he now comes to the mother and her successors with his penis, it will no longer be in surface contacts producing immediate gratification. They now meet in a monetary economy where nonreciprocity, love, is at stake. Inhabited by the mystical body of the father, the son does not now exchange his phallic value for penile gratification; instead, his real penis is now put in the place of the phallus, becomes a phallic metaphor, an imperative sign demanding love, becomes that for which all goods and services are exchanged: money. Phallic value is the obverse of erotogenic use value; it is measured by the quantity of goods of use value which are exchanged for it.

The sodomite in the eyes of Bernal Díaz contemplating the high priests of the Mayas, the Compoalans, the Xocotlans, the Tlascalans, and the Aztecs is then one that erects his real penis in the place of the ideal phallus and uses it to disembowel paternity and execrate infancy. Human sacrifice, common to the principal cultures of Mesoamerica—Olmec, Maya, Zapotec, Mixtec, Huastec, Totanac, Toltec, and Aztec—had accelerated in inverse-Malthus algebraic proportion. It was necessary that the Aztec world maintain a continual state of war, waged not for political domination, territorial conquest, or plunder but for the sake of constituting brave and noble men as sacrificial stock. The conquistadors and their priests heard that when in 1487 Auitzotzin dedicated the pyramid of Uitzilo-

pochtli in Tenochtitlán, twenty thousand humans
were sacrificed. The Aztec order, dazzling and frail as
its lord Uitzilopochtli, The Hummingbird of the Left,
had succeeded the Toltecs whose pacific deity Quetzalcoatl, The Plumed Serpent, had gone beyond the seas
to the east; Moctezoma Xocoyotzin held himself in
readiness to sacrifice resolutely the entire Aztec world
upon his return. In the perception of Quetzalcoatl
Hernando Cortés, it had become an infernal sodomist
machine turning for the damnation and annihilation
of mankind. Hernando Cortés hurled himself against
it, worshipping the Son of Man, driven by his sense
of the value of man, and of gold.

The sodomist perversion, as perhaps every perversion, is a perversion of the rationale of economy; the ex-
changes can no longer continue by way of compensations. The sodomist phantasm put in the place of the
possible utility of the human organism does not have the
phenomenal form of value, exchange value; it is an un-
evaluatable value. The perversity lies in the inexchang-
ability of the sodomist position. Recognizing a sodomite
in the Aztec, Bernal Díaz recognizes a sovereign singularity, a cosmos severed from every genus, exterminat-
ing angel, an angel in St. Thomas Aquinas's eidetic definition, alone in his species, unreproducing and without
kin, an individual that exhausts the species, that comes
to be in laying waste the species. But what he, craving salvation, redemption, and gold, could not understand is that the supreme act on the pyramid of Uitzilopochtli was the sacrifice of this sovereignty in order that the gods exist, that the trajectories of time
run their course. We should not say: that the cosmos
turn, for there was precisely not, without blood, an order that would maintain the terrible dispersion of the
heavenly bodies in the immensity of the nothingness.

Sacrifice of the monstrous sovereignty in order that
the universal dispersion be a cosmos. In order that the
movements of time depart.

The monstrous splendor of the absolute value does
not have the phenomenal form of value, exchange
value. The proprietor of the absolute value does not
exchange what belongs to him for anything he could
receive in return; he gives in order to not receive.
One has, to be sure, received one's existence. In giving one's existence to the universe, has one then perceived anything more than exchange value in that
existence? The reality of the *more* could only consist
in giving more than one is, as servility is constituted
in receiving more than one can give in return. The
giving, with one's existence, of more than one is was
the exorbitance to which the Aztecs destined themselves.

It was at Cholula, on the pyramid of Quetzalcoatl,
the greatest structure ever built on this planet, 1,600
feet square, rising over forty-three acres, greater than
the great pyramid of Cheops in Egypt, that the sacrifice was fixed in its canonical form. The sacrifice was
the most beautiful male of his year, face painted gold,
wearing jade bird's mask of the wind god, on his
throat a jewel in the shape of a butterfly, wearing
golden socks and sandals, clad with a mantle of glittering green quetzal plumes, a diadem on his head.
For forty days he went through the city dancing and
singing; the crowds adored him with flowers and exquisite food. He was given to drink crushed coca
mixed with human blood and peyotl. At length the
appointed day had come. He ascended the great pyramid, lay spread-eagled on the sacrificial stone for the
black-faced priests to open his breast with obsidian
daggers to pull out his heart, and for the nobles to

partake of his flesh and blood. Not a nourishment, human flesh with human flesh: Eucharist of Quetzalcoatl, the departing one.

Moctezoma Xocoyotzin had been completely informed of every detail of Cortés's ships—his horses, his supplies, his arms, his acts. He had sent his priests to Cortés with a turquoise mask splayed with quetzal plumes, that of the priest of Quetzalcoatl. He had repeatedly sent emissaries with tribute more and more in excess of what Cortés told them he had come for. Now Cortés was in the city, with his four hundred men, his fourteen pieces of firearms, surrounded by two hundred thousand armed Aztecs. One day Cortés asks for an audience with Moctezoma, seizes him, puts him in house arrest in his own palace. Moctezoma takes every precaution to make sure that his generals do nothing whatever, he accedes to all Cortés's wishes, including the desecration of the most sacred temples. Each day he conceives more and more lavish gifts of gold objects, and orders them to be brought to Cortés. Moctezoma, tall, lean, elegant, dressed in white embroidered robes which are worn but once and destroyed, adorned with jewels and glittering plumes, the sole Aztec proved not to be a sodomite, is, Cortés perceives, mesmerized with love for him. Cortés trims his beard, practices the most ceremonious Castillian manners, fondles his sparkling gifts like a courtesan, and speaks each time of the great love he has for Moctezoma. He keeps Moctezoma from his harem and distributes to his subalterns the princesses Moctezoma offers him. He must be bought with gold, with daily gifts of ever greater piles of gold jewelry, with armies, with an empire, with a whole civilization. When Moctezoma was dead, Bernal Díaz reports that not one of the

troops of Cortés received a single gold piece from the
plunder; Cortés had appropriated it to the last dram.
His pay for the love of Moctezoma.

What is ordinarily called prostitution is the merchan-
dizing of one's organism, that first and fundamental
object of use value. The term "prostitute" is used as
an epithet hurled to insult and devaluate someone.
Yet does not one become a value through prostitution? There are distinct forms of value, and distinct
forms of prostitution. There are those who rent out
their bodies for wages, that is, for the sustenance costs
involved in maintaining and reproducing themselves.
One does not need galleons of gold; renting a prostitute's body for the night is within the means of any
sailor or student with a summer job. For one does not
pay her in terms of the incalculable value of the voluptuous emotion received but in terms of what any
working woman needs to keep herself in business, as,
in capitalism, one pays a factory worker not the
equivalent of the surplus value his labor contributes
to the raw materials but the cost of the sustenance he
requires to reproduce himself as manpower.

It is marketing by procurers that makes it possible for prostitutes to sometimes command enormous
prices. Their use value is determined by the labor
hours released for productive and commercial activity
in their possessor—one hour of personality N is
worth to the entrepreneur in advertising effectiveness
eight hundred billboards erected along freeways. The
voluptuous emotion provoked in consumers by the
body of Farrah Fawcett or Mark Spitz is worth so
much in terms of shampoo or swim trunks sold. Paying cash makes preserving human dignity possible. It
is the basis of the distinction between those firm tits

and bulging cock, rented out, and the person as such, transcendent focus of choice—that is, proprietor now of the means for appropriation of any commodities whatever.

Sade's *Nouvelle Justine* stages a third possibility: that of being driven to sell oneself, not out of penury, but out of extravagant wealth. One then forces oneself on the market, not as a usable object of exchange value, but as that against which the use value of all organisms is measured, that is, as money.

Such a soul, where venality is pure and nowise motivated by the material needs of human nature, we can contemplate writ large in the El Dorado imagined by Sade.[7] The most generalized form of exchange value, the monetary form, requires that all objects of use value can be exchanged for one item absolutely indeterminate in use value. In the monetary economy being extended across the planet outside of Sade's prison cell, each good of real use value is evaluated in terms of its equivalent in gold, the least useful of available substances, less useful than dirt or rocks. Gold is the most useless metal both by reason of its properties and because of its scarcity. Were it abundant one could plaster one's walls with it, for though it is too soft to use in implements, it is as good a nonconductor of heat, cold, and sound as lime. Sade dreams of an economy in which the entrepreneurs would be paid by the consumers not in cash but in women. The entrepreneurs would in turn pay the labor force in women. The stock of women destined as currency in the economy would have to be maintained by the labor of other women, who for their labor would be paid in men.

In Sade's time English merchants on the banks of the Monomotapa and the shores of the Gulf of

Guinea expressed the value of all commodities in
terms of human beings. Thus four ounces of gold,
thirty piasters of silver, three-quarters of a pound of
coral, or seven pieces of Scottish cloth were, according
to Father Labat, worth one slave.[8] But a slave is an
organism, that is, a living substance organized by a
political economy; it is the first and fundamental object of use value. In order to function, in the El Dorado imagined by Sade, as money, the women and
the men for which all usage objects are exchanged
must themselves be without use value. Simply maintaining possession of them does not liberate the possessor of a quantum of hours to be devoted to productive and commercial activity. They are not to be used
for reproductive copulation, which yields the possessor
potentially enterprising offspring. The time they are
in the hands of their possessor is occupied in the production of an unprofitable and sterile voluptuous
emotion. All one can do with the inert form of currency, one's gold, is fondle it. All one can do with live
currency is fondle, caress, massage, blow, spread it.
These objects are without use value by reason of their
scarcity as by reason of their properties. They do not
have rare physiognomy or charismatic personality
that could be marketed. They have the shape of retired stockbrokers, the charisma of dentists' or professors' wives. For El Dorado is, we now know, in south
Florida.

A living organism becomes currency through venality—when, in a society where all things of use
value are exchanged for gold, the gold in turn is appropriated by one who gives in exchange only the
gratuity of voluptuous emotion. The voluptuous emotion, evanescent and sterile discharge, acquires preem-
inent value in a political economy by reason of its

29

capacity to render goods of use value useless. The
measure of its value is calibrated by the number of
those it can deprive of useful goods. Juliette, through
years of indefatigable asceticism, has made herself
available for any conceivable debauchery. Her utter
contempt for all norms and rights has made her im-
mensely rich; now she is ready to sell herself. She has
nowise made herself an object of exchange value; she
knows so in knowing that she has never parted with
a sou for the alleviation of any case of human misery.
It is a bliss not to be underestimated; according to St.
Augustine and St. Thomas Aquinas, the blessed in
heaven spend their eternity watching the torments of
the damned, *ut beatitude illis magis complaceat.*

There arrived in Seville, on December 9, 1519, the
first ship from Anahuac laden with Cortés's gold—
bells and jewels, earrings and nose ornaments of
exquisite workmanship, a gold wheel seventy-nine
inches in diameter, an Aztec calendar swarming with
designs hammered out in *repoussé.* In August of 1520
Albrecht Dürer came to see them and wrote in his
diary: "I have never seen anything heretofore that has
so rejoiced my heart. I have seen the things which
were brought from the new *golden land.* . . . a sun
entirely of gold a whole fathom broad, likewise a
moon entirely of silver, equally large . . . also two
chambers full of all sorts of weapons, armor and other
wondrous arms, all of which is fairer to see than mar-
vels . . . these things are so precious that they are
valued at 100,000 gulden, I saw among them amazing
artistic objects that I have been astonished at the subtle *ingenia* of these people in these distant lands." In
the course of time the mints of New Spain coined
some two billion dollars worth of currency, and two

billion more were exported in ingots. Two-thirds of
the entire silver supply of the world was eventually
shipped from the port of Vera Cruz. It was the ruin
of Spain. The intricate irrigation system of the Moors,
which had made of the Iberian peninsula gardens
that fed an empire in Africa, crumbled into ruins;
famine ravaged the countryside; and goats sheared the
soil even of weeds so that the topsoil was burnt and
eroded to leave the rocky desert the peninsula is today. Spanish manufacture and crafts were bankrupted,
the guilds were disbanded, merchants were ruined.
The cities became hostages of their fifth column of
subproletariat, the countryside of bandits. Finally, the
Spanish throne fell to Napoleonic armies, and the
Creoles in New Spain emancipated Central and South
America from Spain within twenty years. The race of
Spaniards whose organisms figured in the economy as
objects of use value entirely exchanged for Moctezoma's gold, which is exchanged for the figure of Hernando Cortés. Man of inestimable value.

What did the knight of faith look like? "Hernán
Cortés," wrote Gómara, "was of a good stature, broad-
shouldered and deep-chested; his color, pale; his
beard, fair; his hair, long. . . . As a youth he was mis-
chievous; as a man, serene; so he was always a leader
in war as well as in peace. . . . He was much given to
consorting with women, and always gave himself to
them. The same was true with his gaming, and he
played at dice marvelous well and merrily. He loved
eating, but was temperate in drink, although he did
not stint himself. He was a very stubborn man, as a
result of which he engaged in more lawsuits than was
proper to his station. . . . In his dress he was elegant
rather than sumptuous, and was exceedingly neat. He
took delight in a large household and family, in silver

service and dignity. He bore himself nobly, with such gravity and prudence that he never gave offense or seemed unapproachable. . . . He was devout and given to praying; he knew many prayers and Psalms by heart."[9]

What does the knight of faith look like? Kierkegaard wanted to know. "People commonly travel around the world to see rivers and mountains, new stars, birds of rare plumage, queerly deformed fishes, ridiculous breeds of men—they abandon themselves to the bestial stupor which gapes at existence, and they think they have seen something. This does not interest me. But if I knew where there was such a knight of faith, I would make a pilgrimage to him on foot, for this prodigy interests me absolutely. I would not let go of him for an instant, every moment I would watch to see how he managed to make the movements, I would regard myself as secured for life, and would divide my time between looking at him and practicing the exercises myself, and thus would spend all my time admiring him. . . . Here he is. Acquaintance made, I am introduced to him. The moment I set eyes on him I instantly push him from me, I myself leap backwards, I clasp my hands and say half aloud, 'Good Lord, is this the man? Is it really he? Why, he looks like a tax-collector!'"[10] But not tax collecting, just on a tax write-off: those pale men and women, those values, shipped off to Acapulco, to Cancun, to Barbados, to Tangier, to Sanur, in exchange for all the gold, the diamonds, the uranium, and the bananas.

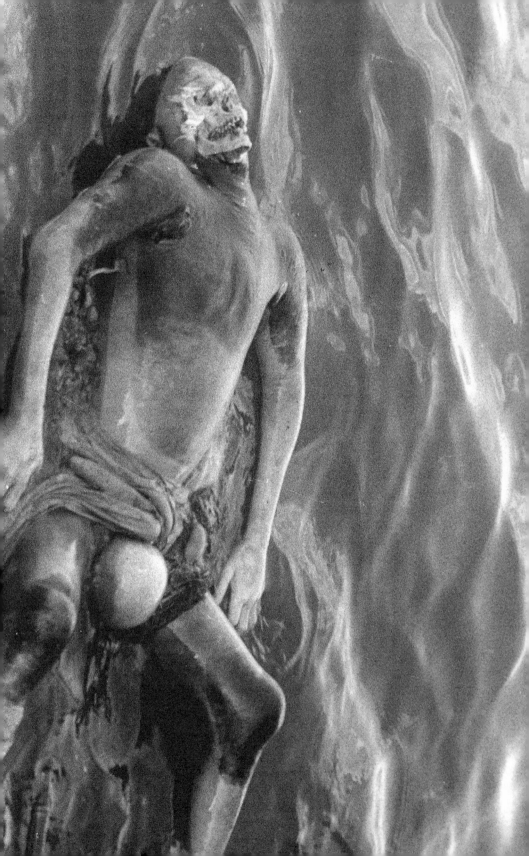

A Doctor in Havana

Speech can be impulsive, ideolectic, capricious, incon-
sequential. What we call speech that is serious claims
to speak the truth. The truth concerns the community. Statements can be true only in the discourse of
an established community which determines what
could count as observations, what standards of accu-
racy in determining observations are possible, how the
words of common language are restricted and defined
for use in different scientific disciplines, practical or
technological enterprises, ritual practices, and entertainment with others.

Every community excludes certain statements as
incompatible with the body of statements established
as true. Every community excludes certain kinds of
statements as not being able to be true. Every community excludes certain individuals, whose basic antisocial act consists in not making sense, identifying
them as fanatics, as subversives, mystics, savages, infantile, insane. One does not answer what they say
seriously; one meets what they say with silence, one
employs force—the force of pedagogy, psychiatry,
and the police—to make them speak in the ways of
truth.

Torture is not simply the persistence of animal
savagery in institutionalized forms of society. Would
the solitary monster be produced not by an atavist
regression to the instincts of beasts of prey but by a
condensation in him or her of violent methods

elaborated in institutions? It seems clear that confirmed rapists act not out of the raw sex drive
stripped of social control but out of the contraction
in them of the institutional imagos and practices of
the millennial patriarchal society. The one who
gouges out the eyes of his victim has not regressed to
the presocialized instincts of apes but has ascended to
the ranks of the Ottoman Janissaries and the Roman
Inquisition. The one who gouges out his own eyes,
who devises dungeons and gibbets for himself, has
made occult pacts with the dark powers of the social
order.

The torturer works to tear away at the victim's
body and prove to him that he is a terrorist or psychotic and that what he believed in is delusions. The
victim himself must supply the proof, by his confession. He is not being asked to declare to be true what
he knows to be false. The torturer demands of the
antisocial one that he confess that he is incapable of
the truth, that his bestial body is incapable of lucidity
and discernment, that it is nothing but corruption
and filth.

Torturers are armed with the implements supplied by ancient practice and modern psychotechnology. They are agents working in the Intelligence
Division. The instruments and techniques of torture
do have the power to render a body impotent and
brutish, tearing away at its integrity, proving it is
spineless and gutless. Modern pharmacology each
week provides new methods to neutralize the organic chemistry that crystallizes visions and that
exudes convictions.

The confession uttered will be integrated into
the common discourse that circulates in the community, and which each one joins whenever he speaks

seriously. The cries and bestial moans out of which it came will be lost in the night and the fog.

To speak seriously is not simply to establish and communicate what is true. To speak is to respond to someone who has presented himself or herself. One catches up the tone of his address, her question, his voice resounds in one's own, one answers in the words and forms of speech which are hers. To respond is to present oneself, with one's past, one's resources, and the lines one has cast ahead of one—offering them to the one that faces, whose voice is an appeal and a contestation.

As one speaks to the one present, one responds to him with the voice of the child one was, of one's parents, one's teachers, responds to the words of persons who have passed on, who have passed away. And one offers a response not just to close the question in the now; one's response already invokes her assent or her contestation. When, on the Himalayan path, someone asks one the way, one's response addresses the hour ahead of him, or the days, or the lifetime, and undertakes already to answer for it. One always speaks to the departed, and for those who will be there after one departs. One's words answer for one's death and for the time after one's death.

Speech can be carefree, nonchalant, and frivolous, its patterns forming only to decorate the now of our encounter. But when it is serious, it speaks for the silent and silenced.

A relay for the circulation of the established discourse, the I arises in the effort to speak on one's own. To do so is to silence the circulation of the established truths in oneself. One's silence is tortured by the spasms and pain of silenced bodies with which those truths were established. One's silence tortures them: AIDS victims identified by established means of research as homosexuals and drug addicts cast out into the streets, Africans not heard by jetliners roaring overhead without dropping tons of the surplus grains heaped up in American granaries, Quechua peasants delivered over to military operations programmed in Pentagon computers, forty thousand children dying each day in the fetid slums of Third World cities, an Auschwitz every three months.

One has to speak for the silenced. But does not one's own speech silence their outcries? One gathers up the words of defiance and faith uttered by those shot before mass graves, one gathers up the words they left with their comrades, their children. One publishes the diaries of Ché. The established discourse, having consolidated its forces to determine things and situations by their death, easily proves they are the economic plans of the unemployable, the political hallucinations of the unsocializable, the utopian programs of fanatics, Maoists in a Peru which is 60 percent urbanized. The documentation of their agonies neutralizes itself.

Responding to those who approach and speak, one captures their voices in one's own, and one's voice animates only the words and forms of speech and the truth of those who have passed away. In the formulations of one's significant speech the cries of the tortured are muffled. Screams in the night are translated into images that circulate in electronic transmitters. They merge into the din of machines and the collisions of nature.

The words and the images relayed die away into a silence heavy with muffled sobs and screams. One's

own words choke one's voice; they postpone the day
when one would lay down with the tortured, to wash
their wounds, weep with them. Even then, one must
speak on one's own. The words that are one's own are
not certifications but responses that are questions and
pledges, answering now for one's silence and one's
death and for the time after one's death.

"Luis is a plastic surgeon and burn specialist. Luis
was visited by a government official who told him
that two young women, one Brazilian and the other
Uruguayan, would soon be brought to his office for
evaluation and treatment. He was urged to provide
them with extra-special attention, for their problems
were of an unusual nature and required utmost sensi-
tivity.

"It turned out that the two were participants in
the urban guerrilla movement in Brazil, whose then
military regime had gained a worldwide reputation
for brutal and 'inventive' torture of political prisoners.
The two women, whose names Luis never learned,
visited him in his office, separately, that day.

"It was not physical pain that Luis's two new patients displayed, for their wounds or afflictions were
not very recent. As soon as they walked into his office, Luis understood the magnitude of barbarism that
had been visited upon these two otherwise normal
and attractive women.

"They had been captured in Brazil and taken to
the infamous DOPS, an acronym for the regime's
special counterinsurgency police. There, they expected, they would be tortured and interrogated for
days on end, as so many of their comrades had
been—many dying in the process, others surviving as
half-vegetables, and a handful freed as a result of

successful guerrilla actions. The women knew that 'special treatment' was reserved for members of their sex—the sexual depravity of Brazil's torturers, especially one named Fleury (who led the Death Squad in his spare time), had become well known. So terrible and sophisticated had torture become, as documented by Amnesty International, the Bertrand Russell Tribunal, and other human rights agencies, that the opposition movement had instructed its members to resist or try to resist for at least 48 hours—to give the organizational structures and comrades with whom the captured members had contact time to change addresses, codes, meeting places, etc. It was assumed that the prisoner would be made to talk. It was only the rarest of cases that could totally resist, maintaining absolute silence in the face of such devastating methods.

"Their expectations and fears turned out to be wrong, strangely enough. After several hours of being made to wait in a locked, bare room, they were taken, blindfolded, for a ride to what turned out to be a modern, well-appointed hospital or private clinic some distance from São Paulo. They were locked into rooms without windows, given hospital gowns, and told they would be given the 'best of treatment' and would 'get better soon.' Doctors and nurses, courteous but closed-mouthed when asked what was going to happen, took the women's vital signs and medical histories—the normal routine before surgery. Fresh flowers were brought into the rooms daily. A maddening sort of terror began to set in amidst all this antiseptic civility and preparations for treatment for a malady the women knew they did not have.

"As it turned out, the women themselves were the 'malady.' In their very flesh they would have to pay for having dared to resist. The 'treatment' was different in the two cases, although identical in purpose. One of the women had her mouth taken away from her. The other lost half her nose. And they were released after several days with the gentle suggestion that they be sure to visit their comrades to show off their 'cures.' They had been turned into walking advertisements of terror, agents of demoralization and intimidation.

"It seems that, in the case of the woman whose mouth had been shut, the most sophisticated techniques of plastic surgery had been employed. Great care had been taken by her medical torturers to obliterate her lips forever, using cuts and stitches and folds that would frustrate even the best reconstructive techniques. . . . A small hole had been left in the face to allow the woman to take liquids through a straw and survive.

"During her initial interview with Luis, she had written on a piece of paper that 'they also did something to my teeth.' But when Luis and the medical team reopened the hole where her mouth had been, the sight was far more sickening than they had expected: All the teeth had been removed and two dog fangs—incisors—had been inserted in their place.

"'We did the best we could and gave her a hole resembling a mouth,' Luis said a few weeks later, 'and dentists will give her a set of teeth. But "ugly" is too kind a word to describe the way her mouth still looks.' Luis's face was tight, the color of a tightly clenched fist. Suddenly, he softened: 'But you know, that woman is extraordinarily beautiful. Do you know what she said after coming out of the anesthesia, her first words since undergoing her loss of speech? 'I will return. No one will ever silence me.'

"The other woman had had half her nose removed, skin, cartilage, and all. A draining, raw,
and frightening wound was her 'treatment,' the sign
she was to carry around with her to warn people
that rebellion was a 'disease' and torture the 'cure.'
Luis spoke little about her case, other than to say
that a combination of skin grafts and silicone im-
plants would restore a modicum of normalcy to her
appearance."[1]

Tawantinsuyu

The planet will be studded with computers capable of
storing the contents of the world's libraries, which
you can tap into from your home keyboard, locating
anything ever formulated in signs with a few taps of
your search key. On your screen you can delete and
combine all calculations, all discourses. Extinct henceforth the tête-à-tête with the traveler, the explorer,
the guru. The pagan learning and language of the
Mayas burnt in 1526 by the first bishop of Mexico,
Don Juan de Zumarraga, decoded after five centuries
on a computer; the human species traced back to one
aboriginal pair, not by faith in biblical revelation, but
by genetic decoding on the supercomputer. All data
on the nuclear winter revealed, not by seers and
prophets, but by digital computation at the Max
Planck Institute and Cornell University. Our brains,
our sense organs, our feelings are now massively invested with information bits. Before going to make
contact, with the Aztec ruins or with the migratory
whales, we tap the search key on our computers and
file in our brains the content of all the relevant library shelves on the topic. A few years ago it still
seemed strange to us to notice all those tourists, not
viewing the cathedrals and the waterfalls by the eye,
but peering in their cameras viewing rather the pre-
view of the snapshot of the urban monuments and
the landscapes. We still thought viewing things directly could tell you something. What could any of us

learn from looking at Maya inscriptions? From looking at an occasional whale on high seas? The viewing
is only an emotional indulgence. All we learn about
these things we learn from our computer screen. The
Antarctic continent buried under glacier millions of
years old, but 3 percent of whose rocky edges is exposed during the six-month-long summer day, is projected by radar, sonar, infrared and microwave scanning onto computer screens in laboratories on other
continents. Satellites continually photograph every
centimeter of the visible surface of the planet, but the
photographs are far too numerous for whole buildings
full of geologists or intelligence agents to shuffle
through; supercomputers will select and format the
electronic pulses of which they are made.

But is it about things that we can learn anything?
What we call perception is not the raw given, it is
informed, formed by signs. Signs are significant only
in contexts. The texts refer to other texts. The history
of Egypt is the history of Egyptology. Physics is a
discourse whose terms and rules for formulation are
derived out of earlier discourses called physics or natural philosophy. The statement "Water boils at one
hundred degrees centigrade" is not a law of nature,
neither decreed nor obeyed; it is a definition. Matter
and energy are not things you can encounter by looking; they are formulas in a tableau of calculations and
illustrated by graphs on the coordinates of electronic
screens. Images are not the faces with which the
things confront us; things are made perceivable by
contexts called culture, the transitory contexts of popular culture or canonized contexts called high culture, both materialized as digital programming and
disseminated industrially. The image we see on our
television screens, on the walls of our homes, or on

billboards is not a copy of an original; images are
from the first matrices of reproduction. The role of
the state is to produce media events which generate
national confidence and pride and the national con-
sumption of images of national products. There is no
difference between a political act and its image; the
political campaign was a series of photo opportunities,
as are the subsequent meetings with heads of state.
The things we imagine, seek out, encounter, accumu-
late are products generated in indefinite series by programs. Nature is the set of images we have been supplied in television specials, rain-forest and coral-sea,
hummingbird's-eye and creeping-amoeba images
whose colors are those of cathode-ray tubes, images
cropped and spliced by graphics designers and made
significant by a narrative in the vocabulary and logic
and rhetoric of the current scientific and technological
paradigms. Images are produced by information bits
fed into programs; as they flicker across our receptor
cells, our minds process signs, our cerebral circuitry
formats, edits, files, networks.

It is now inconceivable to us that there could be a
silent civilization, a civilization divested of all signs.
    What there is left to contemplate is the Inca walls.
What there is of Qosqo, "Navel of the Earth," is the
wall of the residence of the Inca Roca on Calle Ha-
tunrumiyoc, upon which the palace of the Marquis of
Buenavista was cemented. What else can you do to
find the world of the Incas? There are no inscriptions;
they had no writing; their astronomy, cosmology, theology, epics, and chronicles were in the heads of the
nobility who were all massacred or Christianized four
hundred and fifty years ago. Archaeologists search in
vain for statues, idols; they were all of gold and were

the first things to be smelted down by the conquistadors—all but the Punchao, the sacred sun disc of
gold and precious stones, which was rescued by the
last furious Inca assault on the conquistadors and spir-
ited away to their retreat in the Andes and never
located since. The first Inca Pizarro encountered, and
captured by treachery, Atahualpa, was told he had the
choice of being burnt alive as a pagan or strangled as
a Christian. He accepted baptism for the sake of his
wife and children, whom Pizarro promised to spare if
they were baptized. After the Great Rebellion of 1536
and the final conquest of Qosqo by Pizarro, Manco
Inca built a new capital in the inaccessible fastness of
Vilcapampa. Four Incas reigned there until, in 1572,
the Inca Tupac Amaru was lured out for battle, and
hunted down in the Amazon jungle. He was given
written assurances by the King of Spain that if he
surrendered he would be treated as a prisoner of war.
Tupac Amaru surrendered to save the lives of his people, and was dragged in triumph to Qosqo, where, in
the cathedral square under the eyes of the Viceroy
Francisco de Toledo and the bishop and the priests of
the Inquisition, his wife was mangled in front of him
and his head then struck off and stuck in a pole set
up before the cathedral rising on the foundations of
the palace of Inca Viracocha. In the year that followed the Inca nobles who had not been baptized and
given in marriage to conquistadors were slaughtered.
Vilcapampa, never found by the conquistadors but
evacuated by its inhabitants, has to this day not been
uncovered from its jungle grave. Toledo launched a
vast program to round up the people from their settlements in the high Andes and relocate them in the
strategic hamlets, the *reducciones* he ordered built in
the lowlands and about the mines. "It is something

very convenient and necessary for the increase of the
Indians, so that they could be better instructed in the
articles of our Holy Catholic Faith and would not
wander scattered and missing in the wilds, living bes-
tially and worshipping their idols."

There remain the walls, foundation walls upon
which the conquistadors built their palaces in Qosqo,
the deserted terrace walls, aqueducts, and canals of
Inca agriculture in the high Andes.

In 1911 the North American adventurer and later
Senator Hiram Bingham announced that he had identified the citadel of Machu Picchu* with Vilcapampa,
the capital of the last four Incas, lost for four hundred
years. Machu Picchu was built on a rock pinnacle
three of whose sides drop vertically 2,000 feet into the
rapids of the Urubamba River, traversable only over a
vine suspension bridge, and whose fourth side rises
abruptly into the Huayna Picchu peak. The city was
accessible only by a narrow path cut into the cliff
wall, where two men could stop an army. No military
attack had depopulated Machu Picchu; the city is intact, save for the roofs, made of braided and colored
thatching, which had rotted away. A great rock
thrusts up high over all the buildings; it was carved
in terraces and a plaza flattened on top about the *inti-
huatana*, an abstractly carved figure whose function —
altar? idol? astronomical instrument? — cannot be determined, the sole one in all Peru which was not
smashed by the Catholic priests. There were no statues or gold walls, though the tombs were intact and
there were no signs of the deserted city having been

---

* He was led to the city by a Quechua boy whose father had gone to
farm some of the still fertile terraces, a boy whose name Bingham did
not record. Research on maps and archives revealed that the site had long
been recorded with the local name Machu Picchu.

plundered. The contents of all the burial caves, mummies and ritual objects, as well as all the pottery and domestic implements found in Bingham's excavations in 1912 financed by the Yale Club were shipped off to New Haven, and nothing has been to this day returned.

But Machu Picchu could not be Vilcapampa. Its round Qorikancha temple is one of the greatest temples of any civilization, its walls and those of the city too perfectly carved to have been able to have been built in the thirty-six years during which the last four Incas survived after the fall of Qosqo. As the conquistadors were able to obtain, by torture, complete information of all the citadels of the Inca empire, it is almost certain that Machu Picchu had been depopulated and its very location effaced from the memory of the *quipucamayus,* the Inca state chroniclers, by the time of the Spanish conquest of Tawantinsuyu. There are no inscriptions, no carved reliefs on these walls.

Bingham paid great attention to the cracked and crystallized great rock upon which the Qorikancha temple was built, effects which could only have been caused by enormous heat. He searched in vain for traces of ashes of sacrificial fires. Archeologist Marino Orlando Sánchez Macedo[1] has recently concluded that the gold-plated walls had attracted a catastrophic bolt of lightning, supreme evil omen for the Incas, and, after ritual purification of the site, the inhabitants abandoned it definitively, taking with them all its ritual treasures. Excavation of the burial caves had revealed there were twelve times as many women as men. One-sixth of these women were dwarfs. The mummies were embalmed with hieratic ritual objects: Machu Picchu was not a fortress but a sanctuary of priestesses and sorceresses. Most likely the six hundred terraces on the cliffs above and below the city grew mainly coca, to supply the sacred rites of Qosqo.

An entire city whose discourse is irremediably irrational to us, bewitched signs, even if we could recover them unrecordable on our software, impermeable to us. Anyone in search of the world of the Incas can only contemplate the walls of Machu Picchu.

The grandeur of the Inca civilization was in its walls, not only in the walls of its sacred cities but in the terrace walls in the heights of the Andes. The power of the Inca civilization was its mastery of agriculture in the Andes through meticulous botanical observations and through vast centrally planned systems of irrigation of terraced mountain slopes via aqueducts and underground canals; it was this that made the people prosper and attracted more and more adjacent kingdoms to join the Inca Tawantinsuyu, the "Four Quarters of the World." When the conquistadors arrived, they found a population abundantly nourished, working one-third of the year on their own crops, one-third on public works, and one-third on works for the gods.[2] The population, enslaved by the Spanish on the *encomiendas,* land-grant ranches, and chained in the mines, was reduced from nine million in 1530 to 670 thousand by 1620;[3] the Spanish had to import tens of thousands of slaves through Brazil from black Africa. Today the population of Peru has after four centuries recovered to twenty-two million and imports 40 percent of its food; the Indian population stands at seven million, and their diet is 40 percent below acceptable levels calculated by the World Health Organization.

In the sacred cities and ceremonial sites the walls impose themselves outside of all agricultural utility, walls far in excess of anything that the function of

supporting dwellings or defending a city could mo-
tivate. Saqsaywaman, the puma-head of the city of
Qosqo, is not a fortress but a temple, and has three
outer walls 1,200 feet long and seventy feet high built
with stones that weigh up to 360 tons each.

The Inca workers used no metal chisels or saws
but cut and polished the rocks with stones. They
were quarried forty miles away. The workers had no
pack animals (except the llama, which can carry a
maximum of ninety pounds) and no wheels. These
titanic stones were transported across canyons and
treacherous icy rivers. They were not cut at the
quarry in standard sizes and shapes but at the site
itself to fit into the previously laid stones. The lines
of fit are so precision-cut that one cannot slide a razor
blade anywhere between them. As to how this was
done, specialists today have not been able to produce
any explanation. The explorer Colonel Fawcett made
extensive inquiries among the Quechua-speaking people of the Andes today and came up with the explanation that the Inca masons had a herb from the
Amazon rain forest capable of dissolving stone. He
marshaled an extensive expedition of botanists and
anthropologists to the Amazon without finding such
an herb. Nineteenth-century archeologists believed
that the walls dated from the megalithic period, the
age of Stonehenge, Easter Island, Mycenaean Greece,
and Olmec Mexico. One knows the recent speculations
about extraterrestrial colonists landing at the plains of
the Nazca lines, who would have been responsible for
the walls. The Spanish who found they were not able
to dismantle them to build their churches and palaces
concluded that they were the work of demons.

It was in the positioning of the stones that the
quasi-totality of Inca high culture and spirituality was

invested. The wall running the full length of Calle Ha-
tunrumiyoc, great granite ashlars of absolutely uniform color and grain, a silvery blue-gray, without any
alignment in tiers, cut in a jigsaw puzzle of polygons fitted together so tightly there is no space for mortar,
stones set so definitively in position over a twenty-
foot deep foundation of small ball-bearing stones that
a thousand years of earthquakes that have several times
leveled 80 percent of the buildings of colonial Qosqo
have not opened a fissure anywhere in the wall. There
are no decorative friezes or cut rims. There are no bla-
zons or inscriptions of any kind. Spending but an hour
contemplating one of the stones of the Sacred Plaza at
Machu Picchu, one comes to realize the time and labor devoted to cutting thirty-two corners into this rock
weighing two hundred tons to absolute precision to
fit in with the adjacent rocks, and it becomes clear that
the endless patience and profound spiritual reverence
for the stone itself are inconceivable today or in any civilization of which we are acquainted.

The great temple of Qorikancha was not, as popular imagination has it, a temple of the sun worship of
the Inca; all the deities of the peoples of the Tawantinsuyu were enshrined in it. Not effigies of anthropo-
morphic deities or divinized ancestors and heros: rocks
from the Apus, the sacred mountains, emblems of the
heavenly bodies, lithic seals of the sacred itself lithic.

After Pizarro pillaged and burnt the Inca city, he
immediately set the Inca masons to build over it the
capital of New Spain. It is enough to look across the
lane at the cathedral (the Inca Roca wall today supports the Palace of the Archbishop) to see indeed that
the spirituality of Inca high civilization is in its walls,
and that when it was destroyed, the same masons can
no longer build the walls. The cathedral walls which

do not recede inward but now rise vertical in Christian transcendence have lost the sense of the Andes, the stones assembled without regard to color and grain, chiseled into standardized cubes and laid in tiers, cemented with mortar. The cathedral collapsed by earthquake before it was finished, was rebuilt, and today is covered with scaffolding, being recemented together after the 1986 earthquake, in which every Spanish church in Qosqo was gravely damaged.

At Machu Picchu one can contemplate the walls without any subsequent Spanish constructions cemented on them, and cleared now of the four centuries of jungle. One can also contemplate them without tourists, photographers, tour guides and their spurious explanations. It is one of the advantages of going to countries full of what the corporate press calls terrorists, that is, armed guerrillas fighting for the overthrow of a U.S.–supported capitalist regime. Tourists are terrified of terrorists. I was alone waiting for and watching the sun rise over Machu Picchu.

I thought that never again will anything as sublime as Machu Picchu be built on our planet. The eye is unable to distinguish the grandeur of the city from that of the cliffs, canyons, jungle, and glaciers. The plane surfaces were reserved for plazas and temples; the buildings were set on the edges of cliffs dropping vertically 2,000 feet and were designed to keep the people in view of the gorges below. On the top edges of the Huayna Picchu summit accessible only by a path cut into the cliff, there are high-walled terraces so small and so inaccessible they could not have been used for crops and could only have been built for flowering plants to be seen from the city below and that would draw the eye upward to the summits. In the city the great boulders that were there remain jutting up in the midst

of the integrated geometry that regulates all the squares
and buildings; the buildings were built not to domi-
nate them but to glorify them. One cannot decide
whether the savage enormity of the rocks in its midst reveals the geometry of the city or the geometry of the
city reveals the enormity of the uncut boulders in its
squares, streets, and buildings. The stone is not disen-
gaged from the Andes, and engages the inhabitants
of the city, the sorceresses and the masons, in the Andes.
The only worship there was of the Apus, the sacred summits, the caves, the gorges, the rapids, and the cold stel-
lar fires inaccessible in the cosmic nights. In the now
planetwide gene-splitting and gene-splicing, atom-
fissioning and atom-fusioning technology in the service of the now planetwide corporate market economy, nature is henceforth a program of signs digitally
decoded; it can never again be confronted with unme-
diated awe.

Machu Picchu is a work of labor, labor of a whole population, the work of a people who lived and died toil-
ing on stone with their hands and arms and backs. It is
the work of a people who had a reverence for the substance of the stone, a fervor before it that alone could
sustain the staggering amount of time and toil that they
put into matching, carving, and fitting the stones with
such perfection. "One of the stairways is fantastically
wedged in between two huge granite rocks which are
so close together that it would have been impossible for
a fat man to use it at all. . . . Considering the fact that
the only tools obtainable for a job of this kind were cob-
blestones or pebbles of diorite which could be obtained
in the bed of the roaring rapids two thousand feet below, it must have taken somebody a long, long while
and a good deal of effort to carve these steps out of
the living rock. At any rate, the stone cutter had the

satisfaction of knowing that his work would achieve
something as near immortality as anything made by
the hands of man," Bingham wrote.[4] Words of a Yan-
kee who had the satisfaction of immortalizing himself in the exhibition in Connecticut he made of all
he dug up and could remove from Machu Picchu. But
the Inca cutter did not seek the satisfaction of immortalizing his image on the stone; neither the worker nor
the Inca himself marked any stone in all of Tawantinsuyu with his name. It was in the absolute position
of the stone itself that all his devotion and all his
fervor were transported, and it is the absolute of the
stone that remains. In them the whole labor, the whole
life, the identity of the artisans was absorbed without
leaving signs. We know them only as, they knew themselves as, laborious bodies, bodies devoted to effacing
the rough traces of the quarrying, the signs of human in-
tervention, from the surfaces of the stones, bodies becoming patient, impenetrable, indecipherable as the
stones, adamantine bodies.[5]

This degree of reverence for the materiality of
stone is henceforth inconceivable. And this labor. Our
labor has been for a very long time now either ma-
nipulation programmed with signs and calculated for
the economizing of effort, or prestige contests with
one another. The maximum expenditure of corporeal
effort in our civilization is in athletic competitions
with one another for celebrity, that is, for the satellite
broadcast of our name and the data in our file onto
all the television screens.

Beyond the deserted citadels, scattered far in the high
Andes, the people of Tawantinsuyu. Why go? Places dev-
ilishly hard to get to, dangerous. Sendero Luminoso, Tupac Amaru Revolutionary Movement, terrorists. The

army. When you get there nothing to see. Scenery, of course, like anywhere along the Andes, the Mexican Cordillera, the North American Rockies. No trees, empty scenery. Hunted by the Spanish to the verge of extinction, the last vicuñas have been collected in ranches where they are shorn for the world market, cloth made of their wool sold for $2,500 a yard in Paris and Hong Kong. Since the Conquest the surviving remnants of the Quechua people have fled higher and higher, denuded the barren soil to plant potatoes and quinoa, the gritty soil thinner, more sterile each season, each rain. They live in hamlets made of mud huts. They speak Quechua. You don't.

Nothing would, nothing could be learned from the people of Tawantinsuyu, if you understood what they said. Everything they said they would have to code, or you would have to recode, in the vocabulary, grammar, rhetoric of economics, political economy, sociology, psychology, and anthropology with which the global communications network narrates its images. Everything they do—the water they carry from distant mountain springs, the clothing they weave from alpaca wool, the hushed and guarded and coded things they say to one another while keeping an eye out for military informers, the coca plants they raise or do not raise—is determined by the banks in Arequippa and Medellín and Lucerne and Singapore and the chanceries in Lima and Washington and Berlin.

Why then did you go yourself to the Upper Huallaga? You yourself did not know, could not say. See them. Their bodies. No, touch them.

You buy diamox in Qosqo before you go; the altitudes rise to three miles, and everybody who is not born there gets *soroche*—heart trepidations, fibrillations,

nausea, vomiting, you can well die. Then, as soon as
the plane lands, an old woman hands you maté de coca,
a tea of coca leaves which regularizes the heart. So at
once you are in touch with them, and they hand you coca.

The mountains are savage outcroppings of the
tortured continental crust; earthquakes and volcanic
eruptions trouble them. Cold, barren, enshrouded
unrelentingly with cold fog. You see people on the
flanks of the mountains, not circulating in an economic, political, social system: bodies that are exposed to one another and to you, that touch one
another, hold onto one another, withdraw, that stumble, that drop to the ground. Bodies that are in the
way, of development, of projects to build roads across
the Andes into the oil fields and timber of the Amazon, of political treaties about narcotics and arms between nations, of political programs for Peru and for
free trade on legitimately controlled world markets.
Bodies marked to be transported, relocated, dispersed.
Bodies without useful skills, without intelligence,
closed in their illiteracy and recalcitrance, bodies old
already at twenty, too old to be educated, to be recycled in the channels of information and production.

You see bodies bent over climbing rocky preci-
pices, braced on the ground against the cold wind,
laid on the ground by the blazing mountain sun, by
hunger and fatigue, leaning seated against a hut
while pounding corn or quinoa. The very poverty of
implements and gear, of gestures and operations, the
routine of the things done make reading of them too
easy, too immediate; at once you recognize and code
what they do.

The descriptive words—postural diagram, gesture,
operation, intention—inscribe diagrams on the mass

of the body, deliver over the body perceived to the understanding and uses of the perceiver. (Two quarts more blood in their bodies, you read somewhere, than in those of the lowlanders, than in yours, blood containing 8,000,000 red blood corpuscles as compared with 5,000,000 per cubic millimeter in yours.) The words of anatomy, physiology, social engineering, economics, and geopolitical strategy pillage the body for signs. Bodies are disfigured and flailed by words and discourses. The words leave wounds on them.

Bodies of eight and a half million Quechua people exterminated in the first eighty years of the Conquest, bodies expired in building the enormous fortress churches of Catholic Peru, enormous tombs for the body of Jesus. The wounds of Jesus are stigmata, signs fraught with meaning. In the opening of wounds on the body of Jesus, the body of Jesus opens to incorporate the mystical body of the Christian community, a community of signs, pledges, passwords, and battle cries. These bodies you sought in Ayacucho were, are sacrificed for nothing, were not, are not sacrificed, are exterminated. Bodies whose names, ages, numbers are not recorded in the newspapers of Lima, in the files of the police and the army, not recorded in the master computers of the Pentagon where they figure only as zones cleared, cleared of coca, cleared of the Sendero Luminoso. Bodies that press against your language, your thoughts, your bad nights in Ayacucho.

When we look at one another we face one another; our eye catches on to the groomed eyebrows, shadowed eyes, patina'd complexion, the careful framing of the hair, the individual style of facial expression; we look at the ridges, contours, the design, the choreography of eye movements, raised eyebrows, the cultured mouth muscles. You look at their unstylized, ungroomed, unwashed faces, see their faces like you see their arms, their thick hands, their feet.

You see the mass of the body, not the anatomy. Not the organs and the functions, being diagrammatically dismembered before your eyes by their dexterous manipulations and agile movements. You see the mass of the cheeks, of the forearms, of the stomach, the rump, the flanks, the wrinkles, the coarse hairs, the moles, the scars.

You see the weight of tissue, bones, glands, nerve fiber, flesh compacted with the weight of blood. You do not know if these bodies are heavy with eighty years of being there, or thirty years old heavy already with eighty years. Unmeasurably heavy, with a weight that augments with the weight of age—with the weight of the age of the rocks and the winds and the sun and the mountains, the weight of bodies sinking into mass graves. Your glance, your touch which makes contact with these faces, these surfaces is afflicted, weighed down with this insupportable weight.

The hand, the stomach, the breast, the knee give no sign and express nothing, are exposed to the clay and the rocks, to violence and violation. The bared skin and face are exposed to your glance, but you do not catch the signals others may read on it; you see the skin itself. The skin you see is not a container, a hide or protection, but a surface of susceptibility. The glance at the skin grazes it already. The face is not a barrier, shield, or mask which detaches the self from the world, a screen upon which the self expresses only what its decision, evaluation, and initiative determine; the face exposes the body to the world, attaches it to the world. The harsh sunlight, the grit of the wind, the damp, the lithic silence push against it.

Eyes without weeping, throats without sobs, eyes
turning into scar tissue, hands turning into rheumatic
stumps in the cold fog. Each wound, each scar, each
laceration left by the storms, the brush, the stum-
blings, the falls, the infections, and the blows stiffens
the flesh, making it the more mute and inexpressive.
The wounds are only the endurance, the ineffaceabil-
ity of pain. They open only upon themselves, and
upon more pain. They open upon a body that is a
lesion in the tissue of words and discourses and the
networks of powers.

These wounds expose these bodies, these bodies
expose wounds. But one has to touch them. With
one's hands that are organs of apprehension, of appropriation, bony hooks. That are dexterous, manipula-
tive, that conduct, control, manage, engineer. That are
sense-organs, that explore, that gather information.
That are expressive, that gesticulate, that speak. That
are the advance-organs of one's force, that block, that
push, that drive, that pound, that plummet.

One's hands that are also organs of tact and tenderness. That touch with movements that do not direct themselves, that are moved, moved by the passiv-
ity, the suffering of the other. One has to touch these
bodies, these wounds, with hands impotent to heal, to
restore. Hands that, upon contact with these wounds,
lose their will to bend the other into directions one
fixes, lose their will to communicate the truth one
knows.

You see that these bodies pressed against other
bodies enjoy being held, weighed, being caressed by
thick indexterous hands. A pleasure stirs within the
cheek kissed, the hand held, the legs pushed against
other legs in the bodies jostled on the back of a truck
in a mountain road. In the contact there is an opaque

enjoyment that is not the gratification of a mind, for
one has no knowledge and skill to give, no relief to
promise. It is in touching another body that a body
knows the enjoyment of its own mass, its own weight,
its exposed surfaces. The pleasure diffuses in the
dampness, odors, and musks of unwashed bodies, in
the breaths that push against faces like gusts of cloud-
bearing winds. This carnal euphoria has no meaning,
is not a sign of understanding, resolve, or solutions.
But it is not closed in itself. The pleasure is each time
momentary, agitated, always in a hurry to displace
itself, to recur elsewhere. Momentarily it glows in the
hands, in the arms, in the shoulders, in the lips, in
the thigh pressed of its own weight against yours.

One has to touch bodies, graze them, palpate them,
squeeze, stroke, knead, scratch, tickle, pinch, caress,
bite, suck, lick, press, embrace, bear their weight,
breathe their exhalations, become wet with their
sweat and tears.

Tact and tenderness themselves prohibit the contact. Out of courtesy, they withdraw their unwashed
hands, their filthy clothes from your clean hand; they
withdraw their foul breath from contact with your
cheek. At unguarded moments the touch occurs. A
child who touches your leg, a somnolent old man in a
truck whose body touches yours when the truck reels
on a curve. An old woman who stumbles, and your
arm goes by itself to hold her. The old woman whose
gnarled hand grazed yours when she handed you a
cup of maté de coca in the rarefied air that left your
heart pounding against your ribs. Days go by, nights
go by when your hands touch only your own body.
But you know you came to touch them, had to come
to touch them. You touch the stones of Saqsaywaman

their bodies had touched with such labor and such joy. You wander down the rocky paths across deserted distances that end up in cliffs and gorges, stumble, stop, your lungs suffering with the dust and the thin air, heavy with exhaustion over doing nothing, mind empty, hands aching.

II

*****

Body Count

It's the gym you want, not the health club with car-
peted floor, gleaming stainless steel racks, junior exec-
utives of multinational corporations, wives of air force
officers, guests at five-star hotels. The gym is a stretch
of dusty ground on one side of Luneta Park and a
shed where the rusty bars and weights are stored. It
opens at five o'clock in the afternoon, when to get
there you have to inch your way by jeepney through
the streets full of workers packed in buses and trucks.
That is when the shed is unlocked and the bars and
weights hauled out, for them, men who work in factories and live in slums full of muggers and gangs
and knives. And recruits from the barracks, with
tough bodies and no schooling, from the rural areas,
who will never be anything but soldiers without rank.
Under the trees tangled in dusty vines the bars and
weights are the antitropics. Rigidity and weight
against the monsoon-sodden decay.

The young factory workers and soldiers lift barbells in the field. None of them has massive pecs,
biceps, and thighs; their bodies are not packed but
tough. Under their thin and hairless skin, they are
turning their flesh into leather. They loiter a lot,
between sets, the grins of satisfaction and comrad-
ery animating their faces as they contemplate their
pumped muscles. Easy grins that include the Joe.
If this were the health club, the walls would be
lined with mirrors, justified by the need to refine

and modify the daily discipline so that mass develops proportion and delineation. The intellectual need not have feared exposing his scrawny frame to derisive glances of these rutting males; the glances do not notice his frame but only his eyes, more mirrors the young males put around their hardness, their heat, and their pleasure.

"I am sorry," one said with military courtesy, "I thought you were looking for me."

"No, just leaving."

"Going back to your hotel? The Hilton?"

"No. Doesn't the Hilton have its own Health Club?"

"I thought I saw you yesterday behind the Hilton. Somebody that looked like you. He said he would look for me here after my workout today. Many foreigners walk along the beach behind the Hilton."

"Do you work there?"

"My base is there, do you know it, the big marine base at the harbor?"

"No, I am staying at the Aloha, it's on the other end of the Bay."

"Come, I'll take you, I have a motorcycle."

The motorcycle, a model whose name and manufacturer had long flaked off in the rust, jabbed through the traffic. At the hotel he unhooked the chain he wore about his waist and padlocked the motorcycle to the grill at the corner of the parking lot. Then, as though as a matter of course, he came also into the building. The security guard came up before the elevator arrived, viewed the brutal cut of his features and the hard arms and chest under the sweat-soaked black T-shirt, and asked him something in Tagalog.

"I am a friend of this guest, who invited me to his room," he replied in English.

The security guard turned skeptically to the hotel guest. "I am sorry but it is a matter of security regulations."

The guest ordered, "Please send two beers up to my room, Room 635."

"One beer and one milk," the other corrected.

The once cream walls of the Aloha have not been painted or washed for dozens of monsoons, and the bedsheets have been washed hundreds or thousands of times, but the rooms have big windows that look out upon the Bay. He assessed the room, the books and the camera on the table, the locked suitcase next to it, as he slowly strode to the window. The sun had set and the sky was still smoldering over the glazed pollution of the Bay.

"Do you see that ship out there," he said, "the black one? It is the prison ship. Honasan is there. Yesterday I saluted him. My Colonel. I am a sergeant in the marines. It was my duty to be on guard in the ship."

"Honasan? Gregorio Honasan, the one they call the Gringo? The Colonel that led the two bloody coup attempts? The young Turk who wanted to overthrow Aquino before her elected Batasaan took office?"

"Honasan is pure." He pulled off his black T-shirt and moved up close and flexed his right arm. Around his throat there was a gold chain with a heavy crucifix. On top of his arm there was a tattoo, a red dagger in a black circle. "The Shield," he said. The Guard pledged in blood to Honasan.

There was a knock on the door. He quickly turned and sprawled on the bed and undid his belt buckle. It was the room service waiter, with the beer and the milk. The security guard was with him, and stepped into the room. The waiter took the signed bill and the ten-peso tip and both withdrew.

"Were you in the coup?"

He sat up from the bed and his face was hard. "Almost all of us in the officer's barracks at the harbor wear this tattoo. Honasan had assigned the assault on the television transmitting building to us. He worked out all the details himself, and we swore with our blood. But you know every coup, every coup in history, is always expected, there is always someone who knows when it will happen. They knew our loyalties; during the night they sent tanks to seal us in our barracks."

He got up and walked to the window. A few lights glinted on the tar-basin Bay. "They captured him six months ago; they do not dare kill him," he said. "The generals do not know what to do with us."

"Do the Filipinos support Honasan? Aquino had organized elections, a year after Marcos was overthrown. There were international observers, the people elected their candidates."

"The elections are the curse you put on us!" he said coldly. "There are five thousand islands in the Philippines, did your observers go there? On every island there is somebody who, when he speaks, children are born dead and people die of strange diseases."

"How can anything be done for the country, for the people in the rice paddies and the sugar plantations and the logging camps, if the system breaks down in violence that never stops?"

He spun around and strode to the table and picked up his milk. "There are five thousand islands in the Philippines," he said slowly, as though explaining to a child. "On each island there is one man who owns the port, controls the harbor. Nobody ships out rice or sugar or timber without his knowledge; nobody raises rice or sugar or goes to cut timber when the rice fails without his permission. It is he who calls in the troops when they meet in the church at night and burn one of his warehouses. It is one of his sons that is elected to the Batasaan in Manila."

Without waiting for acquiescence he went to the toilet and closed the door. Below, under the street lights there were men shooting craps; on the other side of the boulevard the lights covered with mercury-vapor blankets men and women in vague embraces on the ground.

He came back toweling his face and chest. He untied his shoes.

"Were you born in Manila?"

He laughed. "Nobody is born in Manila. I come from Cantawan. It is in Negros Oriental. The sea is very beautiful there. Foreigners go there, to do scuba diving in the reefs."

"Was your father in the navy?"

"My father was a fisherman."

"How many are in your family?"

"I have six sisters and five brothers."

"Fishermen?"

"They work in the resort. You can't fish in the reef anymore; the government made the reef into a park for the scuba divers. My sister has a motorcycle too now," he said sourly.

"Is she in Manila?"

He turned and grinned. "Didn't you hear about the election in Danao City, in Negros Oriental? Ramon Durano is Congressman of the first district since 1941. He is sugar milling, mining, real estate, public utilities, dock services, printing and paper products. He is 83. Emerito Calderon his son-in-law represents the fifth district, his cousin Manuel Zosa the sixth, Calestino

Sybico Jr. and also his son-in-law represented the seventh. His wife Beatriz is mayor of Danao, his daughter Maria Luisa the Cebu delegate to the Constitutional Convention. Now despite the backing of old man Ramon, son Jesus Durano, fifty-one, running for governor is, according to the polls, heading for defeat. Jesus withdraws from the race. Ramon Durano himself takes his place. Another son, Ramonito Durano, takes the old man's place running for Congressman of the first district. Jesus reappears as the old man's running mate. The opposition candidate is Thaddeus Durano, Ramon Durano's son and Jesus Durano's brother. Who won? Halfway through the counting of the votes, Jesus Durano shoots Thaddeus Durano with an AK-47. They proclaim him governor without finishing the counting."

He roared with laughter. He swung about the room, the room booming with his laughter. He glared at the large mirror that hung on the wall and turned his flexed arms into it, then raised his arms over his head and contemplated the contours of his splayed chest. He took no notice of the other in the room. He pulled off his trousers and studied his mirrored thighs and calves. Then his legs and his fists clamped and he sprung back and forth, his black eyes watching the blows of his fists in the mirror bursting at him.

There was a knock on the door; he threw himself again on the bed. It was the waiter who had come to pick up the glasses and asked if he should bring up some more beer or milk. Behind him was the security guard, who looked at the hotel guest, who slowly closed the door on them.

"Will there be another coup? Ordered by Honasan from that ship? Are you . . . ?"

He sat up and then lay back on the bed again, his arms folded behind his head. "No," he said. "The generals are constitutionalists. Do you know what happened that night when Marcos ordered them to march on Camp Crame—where Enrile and Ramos had mutinied in support of Aquino? The military attaché to the embassy spent the night on the telephone. He phoned every general in the army and air force, every admiral in the navy, one by one. They had been trained in Clark and Subic Bay, West Point and Annapolis. They had equipped their men with uniforms and arms supplied by the Pentagon. They are old men, with salaries of $450 a year and fine houses in Makati and bank accounts of millions of pesos. When Marcos ordered them to march their troops to Camp Crame, all but one obeyed the embassy."

"But Honasan will not obey the embassy. And you will obey Honasan?"

He was silent and shifted wearily on the bed. "After the coup failed Aquino gave the officers what Honasan had demanded," he said. "The officers were given amnesty for all court-martial cases of human rights violations. The salary of the men was tripled. It used to be a hundred pesos—eight U.S. dollars—a month. I send my mother in Cantawan some money every month."

He has had his motorcycle longer than that. Did he earn it on the beach behind the Hilton?

He closed his eyes and his body softened like that of a child. After a while he yawned and turned his head. "You have a very fine watch," he said. "What is it, a Seiko?"

"No, I bought it in Italy."

"How many pesos did it cost?"

"I don't remember. It was lire."

He sat up on the bed. "Are you a Catholic?" he asked.

"I don't know. I was born Catholic, baptized a Catholic. I guess you could say I am a Catholic. Like Filipinos are Catholics."

"Do you follow the Catholic teaching?"

"Maybe whether people are Catholics or Protestants or Moslems or Hindus they still know what is the honest way to live. Maybe the guerrillas of the New People's Army too."

"I am a Catholic," he said. He held up the gold crucifix on the chain about his throat. He dropped it again, and his hand fell upon his thigh and stirred. "Maybe I should not say I am a Catholic," he said wryly. "Maybe I do not follow the Catholic teaching." He looked up. "Today is Sunday, and before I went to the gym I studied the Bible."

"The marines hold Bible classes for officers? After the coup?"

"I go alone to a man from Cantawan who lives now in Tondo. You know Tondo? The Smokey Mountain? The mountain of garbage? He is not a priest but he can heal with his hands, heal open wounds running with corruption, he can make the weak strong. He can make people die five hundred miles away." His eyes indicated the heavy crucifix gleaming on the bronze mounds of his chest. "It is a very strong protection," he said. "It can stop the communist bullets."

"It is very beautiful."

"It is from Negros."

"Your father gave it to you when you left?"

"No, the man from my village gave it to me after I studied the Bible with him for six months. Gave it to me today."

"You are very strong. How long have you been working out in the gym?"

"The fishermen in Cantawan are all very strong. But they are not bodybuilders, they do not have mass and proportion and delineation. I have been working out for six months." He rose from the bed and went to the mirror. He drummed his fists on the flat wall of his stomach.

"When will you go back to your village?"

"Oh, I am only thirty, the Marines want me for another twenty years."

"Do you like it? Do you like being here, like Manila?"

He contemplated his lean abdomen in the mirror, then turned around to answer. "You can go anywhere. I get only three hundred pesos a month. You saw how old my motorcycle is." He bent over, the crucifix hung free from his heart. "You can take me when you want to see the coral reefs at Cantawan. I can protect you from the guerrillas. I have lots of bullets," he laughed. "You paid for them."

"It takes a lot of our bullets! I read in the newspaper that a Pentagon cost-accounting team reported that in the Philippines it takes thirty-seven thousand bullets to kill one guerrilla. We have to be rich to pay for your soldiers."

His bent torso hardened and he looked up with wide eyes. "The Pentagon accountants complain that we officers should lead hunt-and-kill squads like in El Salvador, that don't go out in the woods in the morning and come back by night." He looked long out the window. "You go to the resort at Cantawan to gape at the fish, and Jesus Durano sits in the Batasaan squirreling away your money. He skims off a handful to pay us to go shoot the guerrillas for him." He stepped back and stood erect, chest thrust out. His eyes were glazed over, his voice ran on stumbling over itself. "The CIA says that we only kill guerrillas when it becomes vengeance for our buddies. They inform the guerrillas of our movements, so that we can be ambushed." He was silent awhile. "They say we officers take the men out in the woods to shoot thirty-seven thousand bullets at the trees and then get back to camp before sunset."

"Maybe the guerrillas can't be killed with bullets. Like Honasan can't be killed with bullets. Maybe the guerrillas can't be stopped by the men elected to the Batasaan. Maybe we outsiders can do nothing. Maybe they are too numerous for thirty-seven million bullets. Maybe there are too many Filipinos even if there are five thousand islands. Or maybe they are numerous enough to do something. You and your five brothers and six sisters."

"We can do nothing." He glared and repeated, "We can do nothing." He lay spread-eagled on the bed. "The men in the Batasaan can do nothing," he murmured. "It is the Americans who own the resort in Cantawan, the Americans who buy the sugar and the mills, the Americans who write arms contracts with the generals."

He sprung up and stood in the dark corner of the room and looked out the window. The light from the street dimly outlined him. "One day we will have to fight the Americans." He did not turn around. "The American is very big, and I am very small. He makes a bigger target for my bullet than I make for his."

He lay on the bed. The telephone rang, it was a woman from a tour agency, offering a special price for car rental. You said you were not interested, and hung up. You realized he was asleep.

Matagalpa

I drove my car to the place we had spoken about so
much, the enemy capital. Some six hundred city
blocks of Managua were destroyed by the 1972 earthquake; it must be the greatest single natural catastro-
phe in the history of cities. In the years since, the
ruined structures have been leveled by people scav-
enging for bricks and pieces of pipe and wires for
their shanties in the surrounding hills. Today downtown Managua is a flat stretch of savannah. I almost
expected to see antelopes and jackals, but came upon,
in the tall grass, the steel-girdled carcass of the
former Grand Hotel under which a squatter was dozing in her hammock, while her black pig grunted and
hens cackled in the rubble of boutiques and cafés.
Bees buzzed in the flowering weeds, signaling to one
another pollen and nectar the plants had made of the
blood-soaked earth in which they sank their roots.
Armor-clad equatorial ants passed messages to one
another across their antennae as their files crossed in
the tall grass, like marching armies.

Not every human work was laid waste when the
earth's crust buckled; the three quakeproof structures
of Managua floated like well-crafted schooners over
the rolling plains and settled down again when all
Managua was still. They stand today, on the low
promontory commanding the wastes, the savannah,
of Managua—the Bunker, fortress-headquarters of
the Guardia Nacional and residence of the Somozas,

the nineteen-story Bank of America, in Riviera-white,
highest building in Central America, and the pseudo-
Maya pyramid with pseudo-temple suite on top of the
Intercontinental Hotel, built, owned, and dwelt in at
the time by Howard Hughes, who watched the Latino
city disintegrate beneath him from his temple-suite
windows.

What else is there to see in the heart of the enemy capital? The sharks. I walked across the weedy
desolation where once a half-million people lived, to
the Lago Xolotán. The waters were dark and tormented, but I did not see the sharks. The length and
depth of adjacent Lago Nicaragua brought the U.S.
marines who occupied and bled Nicaragua from 1912
to 1933, after Cornelius Vanderbilt had pointed out
you could sail ships from the Caribbean Sea up the
Rio San Juan into Lake Nicaragua and then just dig
out twelve miles of canal and you would be in the
Pacific—a second passage through the isthmus. The
depression in the United States and the armed rebellion of Sandino finally drove the marines out; they
were replaced by the Guardia Nacional of West-
Point–trained Anastasio Somoza Garcia, who liquidated Sandino and enriched himself on a national
economy that now exported its cotton, sugar, coffee,
and beef to the United States. The lakes were left to
their sharks. In the lakes they are so numerous that
the leisure class, who during the forty-five years of
the Somozas built villas on almost every one of the
three-hundred-some islands called Los Diamantes, had
been obliged, in order to have a dip on those equatorial afternoons, to dig out swimming pools in their
islands. The sharks were about the only irritant in
their sybarite existence, until the Sandinistas multi-
plied in the mountains and the cloud forests and, in

1979, Anastasio Somoza Debeyle fled, with the coffins containing the corpses of his father and his brother, to Miami.

These fresh-water sharks were deemed by biologists who studied the matter to be a separate species. It was explained that the lake is really a part of the wide Pacific that got walled off by some upheaval or other eons ago and the sharks thereby trapped adjusted to the gradual loss of salinity. Eventually the biologists took account of the fishermen who said that anyone in a boat going up or down the Rio San Juan who takes the trouble to look down can observe that the river is full of them, coming and going. Now it is said that there is no prodigy of evolution to be wondered over in these sharks in the lakes of Nicaragua—they really are just sharks.

The sun faded into the gray mists and I gave up trying to see the sharks and walked back through the weeds as the night insects and the frogs called endlessly and unintelligibly to me and to one another. In these latitudes the night falls very quickly; in a half hour it is completely dark.

At the edge of the earthquake zone, I noticed a small hotel. There seemed to be no office, but the front room had some tables covered with oilcloth with a few plates laid out on them. I sat down. After some time an old man in khaki shorts came in. He took me outside, unlocked a door, showed me a bed, pointed to where I should put my suitcase, along the wall. He led me outside and showed me where there was an outhouse, and a bucket outside to wash with. He told me to pull my car up in front of the room and as I did directed me with shouts and gestures. He asked me if I needed something to eat. He then shuffled on to see what he could cook for me. I went to sit down in the dining room. He brought in some tortillas and refried beans. Then he went out and did not return.

I walked down the street a few blocks, turned left, passed houses in weedy lots with no lights showing, then circled back to the hotel. I had no unread novels in my suitcase, pulled out a book on animal communication systems, and lay on the bed to read.

Suddenly the bed shook violently and the light went out. I leapt up and ran outside. The city was dark. But I heard no shouts, only the distant yelps of squabbling dogs, and the old man did not reappear. I looked at the hotel. There were a half-dozen rooms in a row, none with a second floor, walls of thick stucco, covered with sheets of corrugated iron. I did not feel any more tremors. I went back inside, pushed the bed equidistant from the four walls, and lay down. Mosquitos whined; I pulled the sheet over my head. It was very hot and I did not get to sleep for a long time.

The communication systems of bees and ants designate things—they designate the nature of and the location of the flowers and the gums. The relationships that hold among the bees—the queen, hive and field workers, drones—do not seem to be coded in the dances with which the bees communicate; they are apparently programmed genetically and are not communicated in the digital systems of the language.

Among mammals it seems that the communication systems designate not things but relationships. When female wolves come in heat they proposition the pack leader by bumping against him with their rear ends. More often than not he does not respond, though he does act to prevent other males from getting the females. Benson Ginsburg filmed one of these males who succeeded in establishing coitus with a female. As in the other *Canidae*, the male wolf is locked in the female, unable to withdraw his penis, and this animal was helpless. The pack leader rushed up—but did not attack him. He pressed down the head of the offending male four times with his open jaws and then walked away. This signal is that of the weaning order made by adult females and males; the adult crushes the puppy down by pressing its open mouth on the back of the puppy's neck. The pack leader then did not "negatively reinforce" the other male's sexual activity; he asserted or affirmed the nature of the relationship between himself and the other. If we were to translate the pack leader's gesture into our words, they, Gregory Bateson said, would not be "Don't do that," but "I am your senior adult male, you puppy."

Human hands that take hold and draw nothing to themselves, taking form and deforming themselves, forming nothing, speaking, solicit and engage one. Addressing another with his words, confiding his presence to a breath that hardly stirs the air, the other comes disarmed and disarming. The naked eyes that look at you appeal to you and contest you. The skin inscribed with its own wrinkles exposes the fragility of youth and age, the organic dead ends of birthmarks, the languor of eyes that close. One's eyes touch it lightly, with a touch that is affected, moved, afflicted by it.

Pumping diaphragm and tightening muscles refract the eye that sees them to objectives being envisioned or obstacles being identified. The buoyant stride answers to and makes visible the fresh winds coming in from the evening lake. The restless sprawl designates the interminable tedium of the muddy slum. The rigid pace and wary eye signals dangers caught sight of or divined. Human language is not just an evolutionary development of the kinesics of mammals; something new has been added. Not abstraction or generalization, which exist in all communication systems. It is the discovery of how to be specific about something other than relationships. The language of things characteristic of insects has been added.

The rains had come; for months now it would pour over the shark-filled lakes and the rubble and shanties of Managua. I drove my car through the city filled with passwords and guns. One did not see but read the streets; the wet walls of the shanties were not the sides of constructions but placards covered with slogans. The year of the victory they abolished the Guardia Nacional and proclaimed it the Year of Literacy; only 1.1 percent of the population had finished sixth grade. The eighty-five thousand who could read went to teach all those who could not how to write their names before they die. The eighty-five thousand shall not forget those names. But this year the words, written wherever a slogan can be written, were *Todas las Armas al Pueblo*. Seventeen U.S. warships waited off both coasts; the Sandinistas were passing out rifles to every man and woman who would spend an hour learning how to use one. On July 19, anniversary of the entry of the Sandinistas into Managua in 1979, I was able to find a service station that could sell me five gallons of gas and left the city for the mountains up north. It was at the fork turning to Matagalpa that you stopped my car, Augusto.

You carried a rifle. Once again. You had carried it four years in this jungle hunting and being hunted by the men of the Guardia Nacional of Somoza, now rearmed and poised across the border. When we got to Matagalpa, you said there were no suitable hotels here—suitable for a gringo, I supposed—and that I should go to Santa Maria de Ostuma. There a hacienda, whose owner had fled the Sandinistas, has been turned into a hotel owned by the revolution. When we got there, you asked me to drive you twenty-five kilometers further, to Jinotega.

As I returned the night was falling into the cloud forest. The blackness rose in the giant ferns and lianas, over which towered the mahoganies, ceibas, and pines all covered with trailing tangles of moss swaying in the dense fog of these mountain heights like algae in cold lakes. When I returned to Santa Maria de Ostuma, I found I was the only guest. A young woman with Chorotec—Aztec—features, who said her name was Consuela, showed me my room. There was only rice and refried beans to eat, in the dining hall on whose bare plank walls hung a single photograph of Rigoberto López Pérez, the young poet whose poetry had led him, in 1956, to shoot dead the first Somoza, General Anastasio. I asked for a glass of rum. When I returned to my room, I found a paperback life of Sandino written by an Argentine in 1957, which, the back cover declared, had sold six hundred thousand copies. After an hour I stepped out. The building seemed completely deserted; the woman was nowhere to be seen. I went to my room and to sleep.

There was a nervous knock on the door. I turned on the light. Past midnight. The young woman Consuela stood outside the door. She spoke quietly and with an insistent smile. "We must move your car. Please give me the keys." I pulled them out of my pants pocket and handed them to her. She did not explain. She said, "Go back to sleep." As I closed the door I thought I saw you, Augusto, in the darkness of the corridor. I woke from another knock. This time it was you, and you held your rifle. "You must dress and come," you said imperatively. "Contra." I saw it was twenty to two. You were not going to explain. You are one of those who had taken a machete and a rifle and gone into the mountains, turning your back to the rallies, the speeches, the explanations. I glared into your eyes to see what I could read there. The irises were brown-black, the whites of your eyes opaque as clay. A thin film wet their surfaces. You looked out into the night, with eyes that saw nothing, the flared eyes of an insomniac. Your eyes shifted and looked at me as into another night. Nothing of me reflected on the wet surfaces of your eyes, as though I, a gringo, were for you without color, without shape, without contours, without surfaces, an element of something alien and indeterminate and encroaching, gringo power, marines, fleets at sea advancing in the night, spy satellites in the black clouds above that engulfed all the stars. I stepped after you out into the night. A small flashlight illuminated the wet ground of your step, and illuminated also the wet film of your eyes.

Your eyes shift from me to the night, as we walk through the dense ferns and dripping lianas. There is no path, only the tree trunks scabby with lichens that lined up in corridors whichever way the eyes turned. Your eyes seem to be looking only at the small circle of light on the wet ground before your footfall, and something else, perhaps in your inner ears, or in your guerrillero or maybe Indian instincts guiding you like an animal into the depths of the jungle. From time to time you pause, turn off the light, listen. Looking where there is now nothing to see or watch, there is nothing to hear but the incessant rasping of the cicadas and the whir of the wind. You turn on the light again and each time I see the surfaces of your eyes turned to me, and we go on. You are not observing me, you see nothing of my personality or the personage I am under the sun, in other latitudes, in the light of classrooms, offices, streets, shopping malls. You are not, beyond the night, looking for the opposite, day side of the planet, which has taken what there was to see and know of me. I see no focus of an attention in the opaqueness of your eyes, only their surfaces that have singled me out, insistent as a malediction.

You feel your way through the ferns and the brush and into the pathless night with your skin. I follow you. I look not at the vines and the rocks and the fallen logs but at your skin advancing against the tangled jungle. Your shirt and pants are not a uniform, hold no shape of their own, do not give any form to your substance. Faded, shapeless, worn, the clothing of anyone. Your skin, dirty, worn, exposed, the skin of anyone, of Nicaragua. Like your clothing, clothing of the land, of the times, this skin is not your own. You yourself do not know for whom, and how many times, you have risked it. The branches scratch against it, and the cold fog drips into your sweat. Of you I see your cheeks, your throat, your chest, your arms. No frown, no smile, no concentration, no will turns you to me. Of you I see only your skin, exposed not to me but to the jungle and the fog, exposed to this night in Matagalpa because turned to those for whom you watch, over whose sleep you are insomniac. As the shoes half open to the earth and the rocks, the worn, dirty clothing that bares your

skin to the brush and the cold exposes you to the
touch of others, of anyone. I think that this rough
skin has been much caressed, by children, by lovers,
by the wounded and the dying. You are one they
could touch.

Your lean muscles strain through your skin. You
have been much hungry. The rice and refried beans I
ate this night you have eaten almost every night of
your life. This hollow hunger long present in you is
not avidity but hardness. You are silent this night, as
probably most nights; you do not have skills at conversation. Skills with language personalize; one makes
oneself singular not so much by the originality of
one's deeds — most of our acts are those of any human, any animal — but by the singular and eccentric
use of words. Your words are brief, monosyllabic, immemorial formulas of the mountains. This reticence,
this illiteracy, is in you impermeability in the face of
the newspapers, the explanations, the idealizations,
the lies.

"Alto!" you hiss at me, stopping suddenly, the gold
in your teeth gleaming like barbarian jewels. There is
a serpent poised in the tube of light your hand grips.
You are utterly immobile. Then you hurl your machete. At once we move on, the serpent annihilated
by the night. Your machete clears the space for your
speed, hurling away the brush. You do not move me-
thodically, surveying and manipulating resistances,
but in emptiness, space emptied of its contents by the
night. Space emptied for speed.

Abruptly you switch off the flashlight; there is a
crash in the brush. Darkness pressed back against
me; I feel your body stiff against me, your rifle
cocked and hard in the waves of black. There is another crash in the brush; your light shoots out upon a

spider monkey flinging itself through the trees with its long arms. I see under my face your arms holding your rifle. Your eyes have become hard as bullets. Your biceps are cables and thongs, strong as those of the monkey. Like a machete or a boomerang, your bent arm is made for hurling, not to operate tools or machinery. What you had always had in your arms were arms. Is that what you are, another rifle, an arm? You had not offered me your hand, your understanding. Your arms are projectiles, not prehensile organs. Not your hands but your biceps are the sense organs of your body. Your body is not an implement but a ballistic. Your mind is a succession of discharges of speed and of immobility. It is impassive and inexpressive, then your hatred, your assurance, your suspicions, your trust, your contempt break out in rapid discharges. Your affects too are projectiles, arms.

You stopped under ceiba trees. "Wait here," you said. You cast your left arm in a circle toward the ground covered with thick moss, toward the floor of the past. "Sandino camped here," you said, without any expression on your lips. Then you turned and were gone. For a minute I heard the sound of your footfalls on the leaves and brush, but then they were lost in the nervous crackling of the cicadas. It seemed to me that you had hurled yourself into some impossibly remote and prehistorical past. Guerrillas are not advancing out of the jungles and swamps toward the future war, where the annihilation of human beings will be calculated in think tanks and realized by technicians pushing buttons.

You had left me the flashlight, but I turned it off to conserve the batteries. The cold dark fog blotted out the sky completely. The last phosphorescence in my eyes faded out and the night became absolute.

MATAGALPA

The insect commotion, obsessive and meaningless, blotted out the lingering trace of the few words you had uttered.

Finally the jungle turned into wet gray, but the sun did not break through the fog. I heard the crashing of bushes and expected you. It was Consuela. Her face, very hard, forbad any greeting. She carried your rifle. When we got back to the road, my car was waiting. She handed me the keys. We got in and I drove the car back to the hacienda at Santa Maria de Ostuma. You lay, Augusto, on the rug in the entrance hall, your face a muck of blood and flies.

III

Antarctic Summer

Pearly gray and white with a red bill and a deeply forked tail, sea swallows careen in the wake of the ship advancing across Drake Passage. They nest on cliffs, making nests of algae not unlike the cups glued together by our barn swallows. In this season they are in the Antarctic, but when the hours of daylight begin to wane, they scroll up the latitudes all the way to the Arctic, enjoying thereby more hours of daylight a year than any other creature. It's what you have to do if you really want enlightenment. Science knows them as *Sterna paradisaea*.

The passengers ask me to identify myself, situate myself; they situate themselves for me. This one lives in Z, does Y, is sustained by spouse N and kin NN, is making this trip motivated by X. These benchmarks are so many *garde-fous* to cling onto in case of a fall. I sense them turning me into a prop in future narratives: There was even this state university philosopher on the ship! He said the unlived life is not worth examining. They know, as I do, that time is sweeping us all away; we could do a cruise tryst that would make a fine narrative for later. But I think of encounters where one did not even tell one's name, but held nothing back from trust and craving and pleasure, and that will never turn up as stories told later.

The first night at dinner I find myself seated with a pair of Midwesterners who had built three old-folks' homes (in my hometown in Illinois!) and then sold

them for a fortune to retire before they were fifty, a
thirty-five-ish woman judge from Chicago with eyes
dead as pools of tar, and a woman therapist from
New York whose every sentence extended jurispru-
dence to childrearing, dress, and the kinds of mineral
water available in the restaurants of Manhattan. But
breakfast and lunch are served buffet-style on deck.

There are eighty-four passengers who like me paid
astronomical sums for the cruise. The officers are
Greek, but the eighty-nine crew members are the
cheapest labor force one can collect on the planet today—Filipinos, Poles, and Bulgarians. The passengers
are Harvard and Berkeley graduates, educators and
entrepreneurs from the United States and other zones
of the democratic free world. The ship is a floating
colony of ancient Athens, a slave society. On the continent there are more than seventy scientific stations,
where teams from the seven nations that claim overlapping wedges of Antarctica as their provinces and
from eleven more nations that have bases there
search for exploitable minerals; after the Malvinas
("Falklands") war, the Argentines shipped pregnant
women to deliver on their stations, since one of the
claims to territory recognized by international law is
permanent settlement. On board ship there are three
or four lectures a day by oceanographers, geologists,
paleontologists, and zoologists, who tell how in their
bunkers, those (orange-painted) scientific stations
(banked with piles of unbiodegradable garbage), the
field commanders of science are mobilizing ordnance,
manufactured for Star Wars, for the final assault and
unconditional surrender of the continent.

It was only in 1895 that Carsten Egeberg Borch-
grevink made the first confirmed landing on the Antarctic continent. It was only after the Second World

War that aircraft, radar, sonar, infrared and microwave scanning made possible the mapping of the
continent, covered with glacier up to 4,800 meters
deep. Antarctica, invisible, abstract, where the loca-
tions themselves—the south pole, the south mag-
netic pole—are abstractions, never contoured by in-
digenous myth or culture, is a terrain only through
scientific representation. The conquest of this continent is eminently postmodern: the only resource that
can be taken from it is information. The information
brought back is cast in the sciences, without any spin-
offs in art or ethics. Strip away scientific concepts and
the scientific lexicon and one is left speechless before
the frozen continent. Yet the exploration of Antarctica
has nowise produced any revolution or paradigm shift
in science; the theory of continental drift was elaborated and accepted without Antarctic data. The satellites that scan its contours are using the equipment
and the methods already proven on interplanetary
missions. Science did not take from, but brought its
information to, Antarctica; "The Ice" would be a
place to which scientific ideas would go, not a place
from which they would come. The Ice is an information sink.

The ship is pursuing channels between islands, to
avoid the open sea raging under gale winds. This blue
channel is open this month, the captain must know,
and deep enough, but his charts and his instruments
cannot plot the ship's course in the Heraclitean flux
of the fragmenting cliffs. Yesterday the ship found
itself in an impasse, the channel blocked with bob-
bling icebergs. Broken from the glacial flow from the
interior whose mass has compacted them so much as
to change their molecular structure, magnesium-white
with bottle-green incandescence in them, they clatter

like wreckage from an interplanetary armada. The
blue channel flows on but the ship turns back.

Current, float, circulate, flow, surge, outpour express
life and destiny in all our ethical discourses; *torrent,
flood, effervescence, cascade* formulate joy. We have
found our joy and our destiny in sunlit clouds and
springs, rivers, and wells. When I first discovered diving, I thought about four-fifths of my body being
water, three-quarters of the planet's surface being
ocean: how little of reality I had seen and touched
until then! Now I think of the 70 percent of the fresh
water of the planet that is ice, piled up on Antarctica;
this abstract number obsesses me like a cipher of unknown bliss and an imperative. The wandering alba-
tross once departed from the nest flies for nine years
before touching down on solid substance, on Antarctic
glaciers. How much longer I had taken to come here,
but it had been equally necessary. In what thoughts
or what deeds would this necessity be revealed?

Avalanches have revealed mountain cliffs, black
schist and marble, very jagged. I ask the geologist if
they are too young yet for erosion; he answers that
they are very eroded, but instead of wearing smooth
they crack and break in crystal slivers. Behind them,
he tells me, there is ice millions of years older than
these mountains. On their steep flanks where the glaciers have slipped, there are delicate veinings from
drifting snows like the ice flowers on our windows.
One never sees mountain ranges; lying low on these
occasional rock faces and behind them there is always
a chalk-white fog of frozen mist. The sky is almost
continually overcast, not with dark but white cloud
blankets through which the sun soaks in a platinum
stain. The total lack of dust or moisture in the air
garbles the perspective we have on other continents

programmed in our eyes. A seal that looks a hundred yards off turns out to be ten; icebergs that look a hundred yards off may be a mile away. The frozen mist eliminates the horizon, and perspective can have no Renaissance vanishing point. Sometimes the air is so full of minute prisms of ice that the light refracted in all directions erases all the shadows, and you can no longer see the ridges of the snow under your feet; you seem to be walking on space.[1] Cocooned under layers of clothing and parka, you feel only the tepid substance of your own flesh. But the icescape looks cold, a cold everywhere within it that does not touch you. The silence muffles even your heartbeat, then from time to time a block of the ice cliffs breaks free with the clap of a cannon shot.

For days I have been contemplating this icescape without a single thought forming about it; today I abruptly thought of the concept of the sublime. And how misconstructed it was in Königsberg. For Kant, the sublime arises in a confrontation between man and the immense and the chaotic; man measuring himself sensorily against, blocked by, the monstrous, his spirit triumphing in the formation of conceptions of totality, infinity, eternity. It is true that in domestic perception our eyes and ears pattern the flux of sensation—finding an elementary rhythm in the dripping of a faucet, in the waves of a lake—and our minds extrapolate those patterns to domesticate the universe. My eyes have been nowise gestalting this frozen intricacy into patterns; they have been dedomesticated. There is nothing less fix-formed and informative than the ice lines on the rock faces and the cobalt-blue lightning bolts frozen in the ice cliffs abruptly breaking loose and thunderously sinking into the waves, the blue shadows that blaze in the floating

glaciers, this white sky overhead condensing into hori-
zonless frozen mists. Concepts like infinity and eternity are only mental furnishing swept away through
the open eyes. White-out of the mind. The eyes, mesmerized, transported, are no longer mine. Several
times I simply thought how perfect it would be to die
here.

In the sea long beadings of gentoo penguins bound
synchronically out of the water for quick gulps of air.
Then they vanish for a long time; they can dive to
three hundred feet. High above on top the cliffs—but
I manage to scramble up there—three giant petrels
are sitting imperturbably on nests of limpet shells.
Under one of them a snowy white chick pushes up
the mother to rearrange all the shells more to its liking. It takes forty-five minutes as I watch.

The fantastic perfection of each animal elicits a
worshipful care in the beholder. Also in its own eyes:
the fastidiousness with which the macaroni penguins
groom themselves, the fanaticism for their offspring.
After the females have laid the eggs and returned to
the sea, the male emperor penguins fast the sixty-five
days it takes to incubate the eggs held on their feet
and under a flap, like a kangaroo pouch upside-down,
on their abdomens, while the blizzards bury them
with ice and the polar night extends the ice shelf 160
miles over the sea. Leaning from the Zodiac, I scoop
up some krill; in my cupped hand they dance nimbly
back and forth, examining the crinkles on my fingers
with their hypersensitive feelers. I would like to take
them back, create an aquarium they would like and
where I could admire them long after this too-short
voyage. How one understands the station teams who
shot the skuas that pick out the eyes of, then tear into
shreds, any penguin chick that strays! I think that no

human mind can reconcile this awe before perfection
with the vicious indifference with which a penguin
snatches the life of a krill with its rasp-beak, a skua
or a leopard seal rips up these perfect penguin bodies
to devour them. The same confounded mind shoots
up one's camera to click at the sculpture of icebergs
swiveling and melting in the choppy waves, photographs that will reduce them to flat splotches of dye
on paper.

On the exposed boulders, some hundred elephant
seals, young males all, in a wallow. They grow to
twenty-two feet and five thousand pounds. Their flip-
pers are so small as to be useless for land locomotion;
to haul themselves up the rocks they arch and flop
their bodies up like bloated mammoth earthworms.
They shove in alongside of others, but rolling some
of them over, who then just snooze head upside down.
They breathe in short gasps, then shut their nostrils
as they do when they plunge in the ocean. They sleep
fitfully. Every few minutes one awakens, snorts, shifts,
awakening another who raises his head, brawling his
wide-open jaws into the maw of the other.

Above the sea elephants there is the rookery of
gentoo penguins. The adults, returning with gullets
full of krill, have to leap out of the water and get a
grip on the ice. They can shoot up seven feet. They
slide and tumble back into the water, leap up again.
Finally they stick, then waddle up the rocks, search
for their own chicks, which they do by calling them,
recognizing the distinctive voiceprint of their own.
The returning parent greets the guardian one with
ecstatic calls and cheek-to-cheek dances with head
movements as intricate and elegant as the fingers of
Javanese court dancers. The chicks are covered with
thick gray and white plush, but their blubbery bodies

are actually bigger now than their parents. They are
now so big and voracious that when the parent has
no more to give, he or she finally just runs pell-mell
away from them, zigzagging across the rocks, with the
kids in hot pursuit. If the parent can't lose them in
the crowd, he or she may have to dive back into the
sea to get away from them. The kids will be waiting
at the edge of the sea, all round the elephant seals,
for their return.

All the early explorers wrote of the raucous din
and nauseating filth of the rookeries, the knee-deep
muck of guano and dead chicks. In fact, the penguin
droppings are soon as dried, in this sun and wind, as
pigeon droppings on Venetian windowsills. I asked a
researcher if diseases do not decimate these colonies
as overcrowded as American poultry farms; he said
that, after all, bacteria and viruses do not survive in
this climate. I, who do not listen to heavy metal at
disco volumes in my house, but Messiaen's *Chrono-
chromie,* wondered if those early explorers simply
could not relate to birds, like the city slickers who
used to visit the farm I grew up on, with their carni-
vore's ideology of the sloven stupidity of cackling
chickens (chickens, I knew, are a species of pheasant).

With so few species, though in staggering numbers, in the rookeries, the birds, seals, and sea elephants occupy distinct ecological niches lined with
different kinds of lichens, and are not in competition.
As on the Galapagos, humans during a couple centuries landed here, spreading mayhem and terror. But
the rookeries are now protected, like the Galapagos,
and the thousands of years without fear have now
faded out the instincts fear had programmed in their
inhabitants those few centuries. The birds and mammals are not tame; as on the Galapagos, they do not

come up to you seeking a handout. The baby penguins waddle right by you with the same indifference that they waddle by wallows of sea elephants.

No species of animal—not even sharks[2]—is a natural enemy of the human species. But humans have made all the species of animal life in the common planet wild, that is, made fear their dominant emotion. Even songbirds have learned to fear the stones wantonly thrown by small children; even the pigeons in the Piazza San Marco have learned to vault into flight before waddling human infants.[3] Humans are not, despite what Nietzsche liked to say, herd animals. Fear of one another binds human societies together; the state is defined in books of political science as constituted by the monopoly of violence. I visited the Galapagos during the months when the fifty nations of the democratic free world had assembled the greatest military force the planet had yet seen to guarantee its sources of cheap energy.

Diane Ackerman reports her conversation with Roger Payne. "Why do human beings have such huge brains? . . . Human beings dwell in long-lived societies in which they have contact for years with the same individuals and family groups, and these groups are constantly exchanging favors, with the idea that if you give a favor you will get one in return, then you have to wait around and collect on the debt. . . . Eventually the system invites cheating. . . . Then you must become a deft detector of cheating, and if you get good at detecting cheating, then I have to get better at cheating in more subtle ways. What you end up with is a brain racing in its evolution toward greater and greater complexity and sophistication to be able to detect and employ cheating. You quickly end up with animals that have fancy brains.

100

"There are reasons to suspect that the brains of whales. . . . are equal to or of even greater complexity than the brains of human beings. These complexities must serve some important role in the lives of the whales and dolphins. . . . There's something they're using their large brains for that is completely different from what we use ours for. But nobody has a clue as to what that role is, not the slightest idea, not even a persuasive theory."[4]

Will it one day be possible to communicate with one another without fear?

Physicist Stephen Hawking thinks that the Standard Model will be completed in ten years; what will humans use their brains for once their 2,500-year-old effort to reach the theory of everything called science is wrapped up? We will be asking favors in the electronic communications media from the automated technological industry. Meta-physics, which today is the epistemology of rational science, could start already to become cetacean.

The male emperor penguins sit in −70 degree Fahrenheit blizzards for two months incubating the single egg laid by their departed females. Why do they come to the fast-ice of the Antarctic Shelf to reproduce—alone of all birds never to set foot on land—and in this season? What do they, huddled together in The Ice, say to one another during the darkest time of the Antarctic? What, in their ecstatic sky-pointing dances, do they tell the females when they return?

What if this communication is not a language at all—no concepts, no family resemblances, no grammar, no games, no rules? Why, having been liberated of instincts, did human animals then invent rules?

The penguins and the sea elephants do not flee from us because here they are protected. They no longer fear that when they remain in contact with us, we will club them, we will cheat. Will we remain forever sealed from communication with one another?

In the sea a humpback whale surfaces several times, circling the ship. John Ford spoke of the way you hear their songs not on CDs but, like they do, in the sea, enormous melodies rolling and cadencing the whole substance of the ocean, resonating all the bones and cavities of your submerged body. I asked whether there was any way a nonscientist like myself could hear them that way. "Hire a fisherman in Maui to take you out there," he said.

Deception Island is a circle of cliffs, the rim of a sunken volcano. A narrow piece of the cliff walls has collapsed, creating a passage called Neptune's Bellows. The ship hurtles through on gale winds. There was a lesser eruption inside in 1970, still simmering in the flooded crater; the plan was for us to go for a swim in the steaming waters above. But suddenly hail whizzes vertically through the air, our skin is punctured with needles of ice, and the anchor loses its grip. The captain pulls it up, tries again, then again, it does not hold.

We head north, to cross the Drake Passage heading for Tierra del Fuego. The sea swallows join us.

IV

＊ ＊ ＊ ＊ ＊

Lust

The Calypso. It's the biggest theater on Thanon Su-
kumvit, Bangkok's Fifth Avenue. It has seats for two
thousand; expensive seats for the well-heeled and up-
wardly mobile: Germans and Japanese and Americans
and French and Saudis and Kuwaitis and Chinese
from Hong Kong and Singapore. There is a cast of a
hundred, a different show each night. Palaces, sky-
scrapers, desert oases drop upon the huge stage in
outbursts of electric lightning. The Empress of China
appears, seated on the uplifted hands of muscular
men whose naked bodies have been metallized in
gold greasepaint. Gongs and the *shakuhashi* propel the
advance of the traditionally transvestite dancer of
Japanese Kabuki theater. Now the stage fills with
ballerinas spinning out adagios and minuets from
Swan Lake. Mahalia Jackson with rapturous voice
sees the sweet chariot comin' to take me home. Mae
West comes sashaying in with a chorus line of nuns.
Marilyn Monroe resurrects with puckered lips to coo
for diamonds; your incredulous fingers want to feel
for the wound to be sure. Divas, grande dames,
vamps, pop superstars, they are all, of course, men in
their early twenties. Now there is the stripper. With
rose-blushed complexion, under a sunny cascade of
Farrah Fawcett hair, clad in a silver-sequined gown,
she uncoils in the cone of a spotlight. She slinks toward you on spike heels, her lips tremble and part,
her sultry eyes fix you, her silvered fingernails clutch

at her sides, grip her breasts, slide down between her
thighs. She unbuckles her waist-sheath with convulsive movements, flings off her skirt. You slide into
the movement: props and plumage being shed to reveal flesh and nature. But at each stage of the strip
the more is exposed of her body the more female she
gets! Your mind is getting twisted behind your eyes
by the contradiction between the ample thighs, soft
belly, full breasts your prurient eyes see and what you
know. Her eyes are pulling at you with torrid magne-
tism. Finally she snaps off the *cache-sexe:* you see
pubic hair, mons veneris. How the hell could she gyrate like that with her cock somehow pulled between
her thighs? Then abruptly, for just a second, the cock
flips out and the spotlight goes off and she is gone.

This now must be the last number. A big iron
cage is wheeled out by an stout matron in safari
garb and wielding a whip. Inside the cage, a dozen
extravagantly beautiful women. There is a Thai in
Siamese courtesan costume, an Indian in a sari, an
Indonesian in a sarong, a Filipina in a *terno,* a Viet-
namese in an *ao dai,* a Cambodian in a *sampot.* They
are clinging to the bars of the cage, shivering with
fear and weeping. On the right side of the stage
there is a gathering of men, German and Japanese
and American and French and Saudi and Kuwaiti
and Chinese from Hong Kong and Singapore. The
matron in the safari drag unlocks the cage and brings
out the women one by one for inspection. One by
one, each man makes his selection and leaves, until
the cage and the stage are empty.

After some moments the audience applauds briefly.
Then they file out, looking at the floor, past the performers who are lined up in the lobby, their hands
folded in the traditional *wai* greeting.

Antifeminist theater: transvestites are more sen-
sual, more charming, more tantalizing, more seductive
than one has ever seen debutantes, fashion models,
starlets, or British princesses. They are the ones who
have cut through all the inhibitions to realize the
consummate feminine look, that—Baudelaire said—
blasé look, that bored look, that vaporous look, that
impudent look, that cold look, that look of looking
inward, that dominating look, that voluptuous look,
that wicked look, that sick look, that catlike look, in-
fantilism, nonchalance, and malice compounded.[1]

They always let you know. Something shows
through—the lean flanks, the curves only drawn in
by posturing, the unmuscled but overset shoulders:
the body underneath not female though not masculine, virile, either. They lip-synch to perfection songs
of a dozen languages they do not know, but you do
see that it is not these Adam's-appled throats that are
trilling these soprano songs. If the performer has finally had so much plastic surgery done and is so art-
fully costumed that you no longer see the squarish
shoulders or the pelvis too narrow for maternity, then
the magic is gone and there is just an ordinary female singer imitating an act another woman created.
These are not males pathetically trying to look and
act like women; they try harder than women, dare
more, outdo women. These twenty-year-old guys ema-
nating, delighting in, flaunting one-night-stand sexual
identities which we in the audience have known as
destinies and obligations.

You, who came dressed up or dressed down for the
show, feel your femaleness being discredited in this
gala of divas and superstars. You, her husband or her
date, or just there with the guys, feel something ag-
gressive against you in all this glamour and gaiety,

which you, after showering and shaving, would never
try to concoct.

One hardly ever notices transvestism in the streets
in Bangkok; the cabaret is its space. Space not for the dis-
content of nature, but for the specific pleasure of theater. We foreigners, gaping at the female voluptuous-
ness affected by these male performers, don't get a
lot of what is going on, especially when the numbers
are Indochinese female impersonations with Indochinese songs. The cabarets of Bangkok compete in sumptuous costuming and dazzling stage effects; the performers, superlative dancers and poseurs, virtuosos of an
enormous range of moods and expressions, queens in
realms of colored floodlights and canned music, affect
more glorious and hilarious female wiles than one had
realized Thai culture had created and foreign cultures
exported. When I left Bangkok for Paris, I went to see
the shows in the Alcazar and the Madame Arthur
and found them really uninventive by comparison.

There is the specific pleasure of transvestite theater. There is no script for which a director seeks actors who are naturals for the part. They don't do
plays, stories; they just do the femme fatale, the czarina, the college cheerleader, the Brooklyn Jewish
mother, each the matrix of an indefinite number of
plots and intrigues. They have no director, no one is a
natural for a role, each one inverts and transposes his
nature entirely into a representation. Each is a par-
thenogenesis in his own laser-beam placenta.

Primal theater that recommences today in Harlem
discos and rock concerts rediscovers transvestism. It is
only bourgeois theater, which the Balinese think is
not theater and Artaud dismissed as recited novels
and pop psychagogy, that is not transvestite. The female roles of Elizabethan theater were played by

boys. In this theater of the greatest and most single-minded age of English imperialism, these boys were parodies of imperial males. The Queen found much of Shakespeare to her distaste. In Japanese Nô theater, the high theater of the samurai caste which glorifies their Zen ideals, all the roles are played by mature men. Kabuki, the low theater of the merchant class, originated in the red-light district of Kyoto and its plots parody the plots of Nô theater. Female prostitutes played all the roles; Kabuki was performed as an entertainment for male merchants. But it happened that Kabuki was so rich in theatrical innovations that it attracted clandestine visits from the samurai, who soon appropriated it, upgraded it, composed music and text for it, and it too came to be performed entirely by male actors. The T'ai people are profoundly matriarchal, and rural Thailand, Laos, and parts of Myanmar are to this day. Patriarchal culture entered Siam late, through the royal family, which, though to this day Buddhist, in the late Sukhothai period—as Angkor long before it—imported brahminical priests and, with them, Vedic patriarchal culture. Under King Chulalongkorn's program of modernization, large numbers of Chinese coolies were imported to build the land transportation system across this river kingdom; these were to stay on and settle into the traditional commercial activities of Chinese everywhere in the cities of South Asia; today a third of Bangkok is Chinese. They are the second entry of patriarchal culture into Siam. Since the Sukhothai period, in the now patriarchal court of the king, all the roles in the high court theater of Siam have been performed by women; it was conceived as an entertainment for the king. Village culture centered in the temple compounds, the *wats,* which are regularly the scene of

religious feasts and fairs. There popular theater developed—entertainment featuring rogues and outlaws,
burlesquing, as low theater everywhere, the manners
and heroic legends of the court. And working in, under cover of comedy, ridicule of state policy and even
of the monks. Low theater inverts and parodies high
theater. The popular theater of matriarchal plebeian
Siam put males in and out of all the roles.

In the cabarets of Bangkok today this theater has
been reoriented for an international audience. Even in
the cheap cabarets full of Thais, the *farang* tourist
has the impression that the show is being performed
for him. Although every show contains some acts from
Siamese popular theater, in the sound systems, the
disco music, the media superstars being impersonated,
the cabaret is very Western and Hong Kong—Singapore—
Tokyo. This occurred recently, when the military junta
put in by the Americans during the Vietnam War realized that the planeloads of dollars that came into the
country with the tens of thousands of GIs on R'n'R
in Bangkok and Pattaya could be kept coming by maintaining Thailand as the R'n'R place for businessmen
and professionals; today 82 percent of the tourists are un-
accompanied males. After the Vietcong victory, the
junta in Thailand liquidated the socialist and separatist guerrillas in its territory by itself, by decreeing economic enticements to foreign industrial investors, de-
emphasizing agriculture, and guaranteeing a cheap labor
pool (the bases for the Asian Tiger economy that Thailand became in one generation), but also by conscript-
ing the young men in its own army and the young
women from the undeveloped provinces into the
Bangkok and Pattaya sex resorts.

Those who go to the performances of Siamese classical dance the Ministry of Tourism puts on at the

National Theater don't want to be tourists on the
make, more ugly Americans in post–Vietnam War
Southeast Asia. You're on R'n'R, but you're not a GI.
What you want, here in Bangkok, is not some meat
to get off on; you want Miss Thailand. In the sex
resorts, they do not just line the street with naked
young women and men; they put on the beauty contests, in which Miss Thailand wins the international
one year. To tell the truth, the lay will not be very
good; the bodies are too mismatched, and in the end
you will do a kind of pathetic reciprocal masturbation
in the dark. So they provide the cabarets with the
real women, the Onassis and Donald Trump kind of
gal, performing for the credit-card troops, who frankly
can't relate too well to those little Siamese dolls
swarming around the barstools. Mae West, Tina
Turner, Margaux Hemingway, or Margaret Thatcher
come join you at your table between acts.

You are sitting there, digging the show they are
putting on for you, a little abashed at how far they
are willing to go to be sex objects for you, to the
point of changing their sex, to the point of themselves glorying in being the latest kind of corporate-
produced media siren. Yet the cheaper places full of
Thais who have paid to get in have the same kind of
shows. They all seem to be honored to stand in the
dark and watch the high theater created for the entertainment of the white kings. A high theater they
have inverted: the voluptuous entertainers are men.
Might it not be for the Thais around you low theater,
travesty of the manners and intrigues and even of the
state policy of the white court? In old Siam the kings
used to go in disguise to the fairs in the village wats;
the players had to learn to cover well their ridicule
with entertainment. In Bangkok the white kings are

welcomed by the ruling junta—they pay. The ambiguity of low theater has to be yet more elusive.

You do feel uneasy in those places. They make it look so easy, to be a white superstar, these twenty-year-old farm boys from the rocky Himalayan foothills of the Isaan who just got to Bangkok last year. The added gender confusion they put into the creations that Michael Jackson, Madonna, and Grace Jones have made of themselves. And that number where a Thai man turns into a very female, pansy, body, to do a Thai woman doing impersonations, for your AC-DC excitement, of Rock Hudson, Tom Cruise, or John Travolta.

"You there, from Cincinnati, you from Frankfurt, you haven't seen half these your women back home; here in Bangkok you can see them all in a single night. Oh come on, we're all bisexual; you really would dig a blow job from a Thai boy wouldn't you, only 500 baht? What's that? You say, frankly you would from a Greek sailor, but Thai men, well, are just not your type? Okay, just give me a half-hour. . . . Now how do I look to you? Madonna! We're men, of course, but you did not come here to watch the conscripts on parade, did you?"

"Oh love, how beautiful you are, how I wish I could trade noses with you, is your handbag a real Gucci? Sister love is the real thing—are you staying at the Oriental?"

They do try to put you at your ease, these charmers chatting with you so ingratiatingly at intermission, greeting you by name, like your friends already, in the lobby after the show. Yet you leave without one of them. They have made you feel inferior, sexually inferior, not as daring, not as attractive. The next night you and your sisters head for a singles bar, advertised in the Tourism Ministry brochure, featuring

a go-go show of men. Thailand is a matriarchal Garden of Eden. The owner, welcoming you at the door,
is an aged queen. The show consists of youths dancing desultorily to Western pop music who occasionally
strip of their G-strings. They, you discover, hardly
speak any English—selected for their looks from
among laborers trucked in from the provinces to work
in construction gangs in Bangkok. Men without the
apparatus of virility. You notice that most of the
other clients are gay men.

The next night you go to one of the massage par-
lors, where there are a hundred straightforward country girls, seated in banked rows behind a one-way
plate-glass window with numbers on their bosoms;
you can pick one and she will massage, blow, and
spread for you. But they have spoiled it for you, on
the stage at the Calypso, with their last number with
the cage and the matron with the safari suit. The one
you picked stroking the baby oil now on your thighs
is just a farm girl from the Isaan in Bangkok to put
her kid brothers and sisters through school. You think
of the glamorous ones, of the Calypso stage; you toy
with the idea of going back and taking one of them
to your room, taking up the challenge. Taking one of
these guys that dares everything back to your room,
and seeing what would happen, between two more or
less bisexual guys stripping for one another.

Back in the company lounge, when you are asked
about your trip to the notorious Bangkok, what you
will tell is not about the clumsy peasant girls lined up
by the hundreds waiting for somebody to fuck them
for a few bucks. You will tell about having Miss
Thailand in your room for a night; you will tell about
the Calypso—in the classicalized genre of the narrative: "There she was, at the bar, the most gorgeous

thing you ever saw, huge boobs, et cetera . . . and
then when we got back to the room at the Oriental
and I got her dress off, I couldn't believe my eyes,
imagine my disgust!"

It's the show in the world's biggest sex resort, but you
are not sitting there with a newspaper over your lap.
The libido in this libertine theater is not a matter of
nerves going soft, postures caving in, lungs heaving,
sweat pouring, vaginal and penile discharges. The theater of sex is a theater of representation. A woman in Port
Arthur, Texas, with her voice, her movements, her
own concupiscence, had the spunk to create a number;
it is transported whole to the other side of the planet;
she factors out; her very physical nature of being a female factors out. It is the representation of the self
that carries the erotic charge. But the performer—
this male Thai—is there, and shows through, and is
now blended into the act to heighten its brazen glamour. What makes the number the more wanton and suggestive is that he is there as a representative male (his
own masculine personality all covered over, his specific maleness factored out), and also as a Thai doing
an American woman. It is not just the physiognomy, the
swagger, the enfante terrible of the Vietnam-War-
torn sixties Janis Joplin that is being represented; it is
a Thai representing her that is being represented, representing inevitably with himself the position of low
theater with respect to the ruling icons and effigies, representing economic and cultural subordination, representing a certain moment of geopolitical history—
smelted into an erotic trope. You went for the charge,
but to those who hold themselves to be serious cultural travelers and not gross tourists and who go to the
performances of Siamese classical dance you now say:

if you really want to know about Thailand go to the cabarets!

It is the specifically erotic figure, and not the classical dancers, that has this representational power, because it implicates you. Not only because the cabaret show is also the presentation of the charms of the escorts all of whom are available to you to take back to your hotel, but because even while you are sitting there just watching the show you feel yourself being challenged to an intercontinental sexual duel. The decent theater is spectator theater; on the stage of the National Theater or in the restaurant of the Oriental Hotel, jeweled and masked courtesans pursue their dangerous liaisons, from which the decorous hands of time have disentangled the foreign voyeurs—as well as the ushers, the maitre d', the waitresses, and the performers themselves.

When you splash cologne over the greasy pores of your carnivorous body, take out the more rakish of your shirts from the suitcase, go and pay for the ticket, speaking English to the teller, your credit card, your shirt and your boutique-bought dress, and your suave and unflappable manners are so many props in the theater of libido. All your words are phallic or lambda symbols; if you mention the plane to Hong Kong you have to catch tomorrow, speak of the comfort of the Oriental Hotel, if you answer, when they ask, what company you work for, or what university, all this is so many tropes in the rhetoric of seduction.

The farm boys from the Isaan whose libido can be contained within the confines of village possibilities and constraints are in Bangkok for a few years working on construction gangs or in the sweatshops; it is those with excess sensuality who are working out in

gyms, in dance classes, grooming themselves, cultivat-
ing suggestive gestures, learning English, learning the
rhetoric of seduction. This cabaret superstar is a representative of a backward Isaan economy whose only
productive resources are bodies, the unreproductive
bodies of the Bangkok sex theater; you are a representative of a productive economy that produces profes-
sionally qualified bodies, assets with which you ac-
quire productive wealth. It could be that you are
challenged by his provocations and feel a lascivious
urge to take him up on it: After the show, in my hotel room Mr. Cincinnati and Miss Bangcock! Frau
Frankfurt und Kuhn Butterfly!

The libido makes the self a representative. Libido is
not nostalgia for, and pleasure in, carnal contact. One
was a part of another body, one got born, weaned,
castrated. The libido does not adhere to the present,
but bounds toward the absent, the future; it extends
an indefinite dimension of time. What makes this
craving insatiable is the way back blocked: the way
back to symbiotic immediate gratification. Libidinal
impulses are not wants and hungers but insatiable
compulsions, sallies of desire, which is desire for infinity, for Jacques Lacan's *l'objet a*. It is libidinous
desire that stations the self in the Oedipal theater, in
the polis, on the field of objectives which is the objective universe and which is the universe of objectives
of desire, in the world market, in *le symbolique*.

If our libido is a part of ourselves, the libidinous
gesture or move, reaching for the universe of desire,
represents the whole self. Psychoanalytic pansexual-
ism turns into a science of the subject.[2] And the self
is a representative of *le nom-du-père*, the Oedipal theater, the reason and the law, the corporate state, the

cybernetic digital communication chains, the West. The libidinous gesture or move transacts with another, not for discharge into a set of carnal orifices, but for another libidinous gesture which is a representative of another self, a representative of another reason and law, transnational corporation, corporate state, continent. The love one knows is the gift from the other of what the other does not have.

One would have to read the libido, see it in its context, interpret it. Our phenomenology of sex is an interpretation of intentionalities, representatives, a decoding of barred objectives of desire, a transcription of dyadic oppositions, an inscription of *différance.* Tracking it down we end up, like Plato, finding the whole of culture—including its technology and its relationship with the material, the electromagnetic universe. Lately we have also been doing a machinics of libidinal bodies, a mechanic's analysis of what the parts are, the couplings, how they work, what they produce.[3] We find, with Ballard in *Crash,*[4] our landscape of automobiles, high-rises, MIRV missiles, and computer banks very sexy, representative of our own libidinal machinery. We have also been doing, with Lyotard,[5] a microanalysis of freely mobile excitations, inductions and irradiations, and bound excitations, representing our erotogenic surface as an electromagnetic field. The I or the *Ça* (the Id) that is aroused in the Calypso is a representative of *le nom-du-père,* of the phallus, of the text of culture, the technological industry, the electromagnetic universe. Intelligent talk about sexual transactions among us is talk about transactions with representatives of the self.

But on stage at the Calypso you caught sight of something else—the body underneath not female and not virile either, the pelvis too narrow to harbor a fetus, the lean and unmuscled thighs, the still adolescent shoulders: the indeterminate carnality. You remember passing by this young guy in jeans and sneakers heading for the backstage entrance. That body, now slippery with greasepaint and sweat, belly cicatrized from the tight plastic belt, feet raw in the spike heels, troubles you. He came from a rice paddy in the Isaan, you came from a farm in Illinois, a working-class apartment in Cincinnati. If one could somehow join, immerse oneself in the physical substance of that body, one would have a feel for the weight and the buoyancy, the swish and the streaming, the smell and the incandescence of the costumes, masks, castes, classes, cultures, nations, economies, continents that would be very different from understanding the signs, emblems, allusions, references, implications. Something in you would like to know how it feels to be that bare mass of indeterminate carnality being stuck in spike heels, sheathed in metallized dress, strapped to a crackling fiberglass wig, become phosphorescent in a pool of blazing light. Something which is the stirrings of lust.

Lust does not know what it is. The mouth lets go of the chain of its sentences, rambles, giggles, the tongue spreads its wet out over the lips. The hands that caress move in random detours with no idea of what they are looking for, grasping and probing without wanting an end. The body tenses up, hardens, heaves and grapples, pistons and rods of a machine that has no idea of what it is trying to produce. Then it collapses, leaks, melts. There is left the coursing of the trapped blood, the flush of heat, the spirit vaporizing in exhalations.

There is the horrible in lust, and lust in the fascination with the domain of horror. The landscape

of horror is strewn with Hieronymus Bosch and Salvador Dali bodies with faces softening and oozing out
of their shapes, limbs going limp and shriveling like
detumescent penises, their extremities melting and
evaporating, flesh draining off the bones, bones crum-
bling in the sands. This horror, which does not trouble our minds which compulsively fix substances in
their boundaries and in their material states, troubles
us in our loins. Lust is the dissolute ecstasy by which
the body's glands, entrails, and sluices ossify and fos-
silize, by which its ligneous, ferric, coral state gelati-
nizes, curdles, dissolves, and vaporizes.

Muslims say they have to veil their women in public, because when lust stirs it takes over the whole of
a woman's body. Arnold Schwarzenegger, to those who
objected that most women really don't find these Co-
nan the Barbarian bodies sexy, and anyhow how could
anyone get it up spending as much time in the gym hoist-
ing barbells as you do, answered, "Pumping iron is better than humping a woman; I am coming in my whole
body!" The orgasm continues in the jacuzzi where
the hard wires of the motor nerves dissolve into sweat
and the pumped muscles float like masses of jelly.

Lust is flesh becoming bread and wine and bread and
wine becoming flesh. It is the posture that no longer
holds, the bones turning into gum. It is the sinews and
muscles becoming gland—lips blotting out their muscular enervations and becoming loose and wet as labia, chest becoming breast, thighs lying there like
more penises, stroked like penises, knees fingered like
montes veneris. It is glands stiffening and hardening,
becoming bones and rods and then turning into ooze
and vapors and heat. Eyes clouding and becoming wet
and spongy, hair turning into webs and gleam, fingers becoming tongues, wet glands in orifices.

The supreme pleasure we can know, Freud said, and the model for all pleasure, orgasmic pleasure, comes when an excess tension confined, swollen, compacted is abruptly released; the pleasure consists in a passage into the contentment and quiescence of death. Is not orgasm instead the passage into the uncontainment and unrest of mire, fluid, and fog—pleasure in exudations, secretions, exhalations? Voluptuous pleasure is not the Aristotelian pleasure that accompanies a teleological movement that triumphantly reaches its objective. Voluptuous pleasure engulfs and obliterates purposes and directions and any sense of where it itself is going; it surges and rushes and vaporizes and returns.

To be sure, blond hair represents for Thais as for Nietzsche the master race, candlelight and wine represent grand-bourgeois distinction and raffinement, leather represents hunters and outlaws, diamonds represent security forever. But lust cleaves to them differently. Encrusting one's body with stones and silver or steel, polishing one's skin like alabaster, sinking into marble bathtubs full of champagne or into the soft mud of rice paddies, feeling the ostrich plumes or the algae tingling one's flesh like nerves, dissolving into perfumed air and into flickering twilight, lust surges through a body in transubstantiation.

Libidinous eyes are quick, agile, penetrating, catching onto the undertones, allusions, suggestiveness of the act—responding to the provocation in the Janis Joplin number being done by a male Thai, the looks are parries in the intercontinental sex duel. The eyes of lust idolize and fetishize the representation, metallize the crepe the performer has covered himself with, marbleize the powdered poses of the face and arms, enflame the body strapped in those incandescent belts and boots. About the materialization of these idols and fetishes, there is radioactive leakage; the castes, classes, cultures, nations, economies collapse in intercontinental meltdown. Wanton hands liquefy the dyadic oppositions, vaporize all the markers of *différance* into a sodden and electric atmosphere.

Lust does not represent the self to another representative; it makes contact with organic and inorganic substances that function as catalysts for its transubstantiations. Lust does not transact with the other as representative of the male or female gender, a representative of the human species; it seeks contact with the hardness of bones and rods collapsing into glands and secretions, with the belly giggling into jelly, with the smegmic and vaginal swamps, with the musks and the sighs. We fondle animal fur and feathers and both they and we get aroused, we root our penis in the dank humus flaking off into dandelion fluff, we caress fabrics, cum on silk and leather, we hump the seesaw and the horses and a Harley-Davidson. Lust stirs as far as does Heidegger's *care* which extends to earth and the skies and all mortal and immortal beings in thinking, building, dwelling—muddying the light of thought, vaporizing its constructions, petrifying its ideas into obsessions and idols, sinking all that is erect and erected back into primal slime, decreating all dwelling into the Deluge that rises. It is lust that, in Tournier's novel *Friday*, embraces Robinson Crusoe in the araucaria tree:

> He continued to climb, doing so without difficulty and with a growing sense of being the prisoner, and in some sort a part, of a vast and infinitely ramified structure flowing upward through the trunk with its reddish bark and spreading in countless large and lesser branches, twigs, and

shoots to reach the nerve ends of leaves, triangu-
lar, pointed, scaly, and rolled in spirals around the
twigs. He was taking part in the tree's most unique
accomplishment, which is to embrace the air with
its thousand branches, to caress it with its million
fingers. . . . 'The leaf is the lung of the tree which
is itself a lung, and the wind is its breathing,'
Robinson thought. He pictured his own lungs
growing outside himself like a blossoming of pur-
ple-tinted flesh, living polyparies of coral with
pink membranes, sponges of human tissue. . . . He
would flaunt that intricate efflorescence, that bou-
quet of fleshy flowers in the wide air, while a tide
of purple ecstasy flowed into his body on a stream
of crimson blood.[6]

Lust is not a movement issuing from us and terminating in the other. It is the tree that draws Robinson, holds him, caresses his breath with its million
fingers. "The sea that rises with my tears"—obsessive
line of a lovesong in Gabriel Garcia Marquez's novel
In Evil Hour.[7] Lust of the sea, of the polyps liquefy-
ing the coral cliffs, of the rain dissolving the temples
of Khajuraho, of the powdery gypsy moths disinte-
grating the oak forests, of the winter winds crystallizing the air across the windowpanes.

There is a specific tempo of the surges and relapses of lust, there is a specific duration to transubstantiations. For the sugar to melt, *il faut la durée.*
But the turgid time of the wanton contact is not the
time extended by society. The associations that form
society first establish an extended time in which the
carnal pleasure of contact with another can be inter-
rupted and resumed. This time is a line of dashes in
which compensations for what is spent in catalyzing

another become possible, an extended time in which the water that is turned into wine and consumed can be turned back into water once again.

In society one associates with another—for portions of the other, for the semen, vaginal fluids, milk of the other.[8] The association first extends an interval of time in which one portion can be poured after the other. Transubstantiations become transactions, become coded, become claims, to be redeemed across time, claims maintained in representations.

One associates with another—for parts of the other, for the tusks set in his nostrils, the fangs implanted in his ears, the plumes arrayed in the hair of this lord of the jungle who has incorporated the organs of the most powerful beasts of prey into his body. The association extends a stretch of time in which the transfer of these detachable body parts of his bionic body into yours can be delayed, a time in which the representation of self and the representation of the other forms.

One associates with another—for prestige objects, for productive commodities; one transacts with representatives of oneself and of the other. The association extends the infinite time of the libido, of desire which is desire for the infinite. A time to transact with the phallic objectives, the transnational corporation, the corporate state, the continent of which one is a representative.

When, in the midst of social transactions, there is contact with the substance of the other, and lust breaks through, it breaks up the extended time of association with its clamorous urgency. But sometimes the extended time of society of itself disintegrates.

Lust throws one convulsively to the other; its surges and relapses break through the time of transactions to extend the time of transubstantiations. Shall we conceive of the transaction with representatives of self to function to postpone, control, exclude, suppress the surgings of lust?

Theater, which represents transactions with representatives of self, represents society to itself, but also opens up a space of its own outside society. In its absolute form, transvestite theater, does it travesty, parody, undermine, consume all our representatives of self, in an implosion of all our simulacra, leaving, as Baudrillard says,[9] the absolute of death alone on the stage? Or darkening a space for the naked surgings and relapses of lust?

There is something not said in the absolute, transvestite theater, where one dares everything. Is it transposing or releasing, subverting or trumpeting lust? That is its secret. The power to keep its secrets is the secret of its power.

Secrecy can be a force that exalts and sanctifies ritual knowledge. It can function to maintain the identity and solidarity of a group. The secrecy of individuals can determine the division of labor. The power to deny access to knowledge can constitute certain individuals or groups into subordinates. Secrecy can be a force to maintain a friendship on a certain level and in a certain style; I may choose not to reveal what I did last night, not because I did anything that you should or would object to were I to explain the whole context, but because I choose to avoid a confrontational relationship with you, I value the affable and ingenuous tone of our interaction, where each of us spontaneously connects with what the other says. The one who can say and also not say can make intentions and instincts that circulate at large his or her own.

The established practice of reserve makes it hard to confront liars, and thus maintains a social space for different compounds of knowledge, fantasy, and ritual behavior. To lose face for a Thai is not simply to feel embarrassment; it is to feel loss of one's defining membership in overlapping groups and loss of the social attributes of position. The importance of keeping up appearances, and of the presentation of respectfulness, unobtrusiveness, calmness, of avoiding saying things in opposition to what is expected not only organizes social interaction but penetrates even into the psychological attitudes of Thais toward themselves. "This attitude may go so far as his not wanting to engage in a private self-analysis whose result might be inimical to his own self-image."[10]

The walls of secrecy fragment our social identity. One is not the same person in sacred and in profane places, in crowds and behind closed doors, in the day and in the night; one is not the same person before different interlocutors. There are politico-economic motives that enjoin us each to be individuals, enduring integral subjects of attribution and responsibility. The immense field of ephemeral insights, fantasies, impulses, and intentions that link up in disjointed systems are forced to somehow form an individual whole in our bodies.

Our theories continue to conceive this whole either as an isomorphism between strata, a distributive organization of different behaviors for different contexts, or a dialectical sublation of each partial structure and phase in the succeeding one. But these paradigms do not succeed in making intelligible our *personal identity*. The intrapsychic organization, whether isomorphic, distributive, or dialectical, would be something general. It would give us the identity of a minor, a father, a person, subject of rights and obligations, a citizen, a chicano or a Wasp. But for each of us, our personal identity is not simply a molecular formula of continual knowledge and skills; it is a singular compound of fragmentary systems of knowledge, incomplete stocks of information and discontinuous paradigms, disjointed fantasy fields, personal repetition cycles, and intermittent rituals.

In what psychoanalysis catalogued as multiple personality disorder, two or more persons inhabit the same body. But when Freud identified the unconscious, an infantile and nocturnal self that does not communicate with the public and avowed self, he generalized the phenomenon of multiple personality disorder, no longer a rare and aberrant case, but the case of each of us. Then one can drop the notion of "disorder"; a division of one's psychic forces, each system dealing with its own preoccupations, noncommunicating with the others, may work quite well. Rather than deal with all her problems with the integral array of her methods and skills, the self-assured office manager closes off the rape victim she also is and will be exclusively when she walks out of the office at night. The wall of sleep falls over our responsibilities of the day, and our infantile self is free to explore again the tunnels on the other side of the mirror.

Freud first explained the split in each of us by the concept of repression; the content of the unconscious would be produced by a censorship that represses representations from consciousness. But repression proves to be a shifty concept. In order to repress a representation, the censorship would have to represent that representation; repression is a contradiction in terms or an infinite regress. The censorship the child installs within himself is an interiorization of the decrees of

the father. But why does the father repress? Because
he was repressed as a child. Another infinite regress.
Freud saw that he was left with the fact that there is
repression in the human species and the enigma of
that fact. If we recognize the vacuous nature of the
explanation by repression, we are left with these multiple psychic systems in our body, and walls of noncommunication between them. These walls of secrecy
function in multiple ways.

It is one of the functions of walls of secrecy to
maintain a space where quite discontinuous, noncommunicating, nonreciprocally sublating, noncoordinated
systems can coexist. A space where episodic systems can
exist, where phases of one's past and of one's future
can be still there, untransformed and unsublated. Behind multiple generic identities, each of us builds his
or her personal identity with inner walls of secrecy.

It is too simplistic to suppose that the libidinous
desire in us—which represents the self and makes
the self a representative which transacts with representatives of others who are representatives—functions to suppress, control, or mask the lustful body
surging and relapsing in its transubstantiations. The
noncommunication between libidinous desire and lustful transubstantiations can function to maintain the
identity and solidarity of one's libidinal representation
of self, to exalt and consecrate it. It can function to
establish a division of labor between libidinous desire
and lust, each in its own sphere and time. It can
function to maintain an intrapsychic space for different compounds of knowledge, fantasy, and repetition
compulsions.

Desire is desire for the absent, for infinity; libidinous eyes are quick, agile, penetrating, catching
onto the undertones, allusions, suggestivenesses,

crossindexing. They are also superficial; they see the representation of a self and the self that is a representative. If they do not penetrate the wall without graffiti behind which lust pursues its transubstantiations, this wall may not at all function to exclude and to repress. It may function to maintain a nonconfrontational coexistence of different sectors of oneself. One may value an affable relationship with the beast within oneself. One may not want to penetrate behind that wall, not out of horror and fear of what lies behind, but because one may choose to be astonished at the strange lusts contained within oneself. One may want the enigmas and want the discomfiture within oneself.

After the Sambódromo

Carnaval in Rio. In the Sambódromo, the great *esco-las de samba* parade, dusk to dawn, for four nights. Each escola announces its arrival at the far end of the Sambódromo by first making the night pound and the stars dance with fireworks. The samba begins, the song is sung a cappella during the whole length of the time of the passage. Each escola consists of from two to five thousand dancers. They dance in massed groups, *alas*, separated by duos of banner-bearers do-ing intricate dances at speeds the eye cannot follow, enormous floats called *alegorias*, and *passistas*—mula-tas on spike heels and men doing gymnastic feats. Massed banks of older women in bouffant hoop skirts twirl, each alternating the direction of the next one, as they dance. They are called *baianas*, recalling the women who came from Salvador de Bahia in the last century; it was from their macumba-trance proces-sions in the streets of Rio that Carnaval evolved. The *bateria*—percussion band of two to four hundred, with drums, cymbals, tambourines, and instruments of African origin—is in the middle; by the time it has arrived at the bank of the bleachers where you are, it has risen up to overwhelm the samba song and it is impossible to sit; everyone in the bleachers is dancing.

Our idea of a parade is a representation of society; there are the flag-bearers, the veterans of foreign wars, the mayor and police chief, the firemen, the nurses, the football team; there are enormous advertisements

of sponsors. Here, none of that. The escolas are from
the slums, the *favelas*, not from the glittering high-
rise districts of Ipanema and Barra da Tijuca. Not even
the master of ceremonies, choreographers, or funders
are in the parade.

The escola is a whole theater; the theme sung in
the samba is developed by the succession of banks of
massed dancers and the alegorias. The theme of this
year's grand-prize escola was water—the water of
the ocean, of the Amazon, of cascades and waterfalls,
wells and ponds, showers and storms. The dancers
danced the beauty and the joy of water. Carnaval is
about nothing but the joy of beauty and the beauty of
joy. My dentist told me that he too had danced in the
Sambódromo; you have to, it is an exhilaration that
nothing else in life on earth can give.

People in the slums will put aside a few cruzeiros
a month for years for a costume to be able once in
their lives to dance the samba. The splendor of the
costumes, used but once, is astonishing; one has seen
the like only in the Follies Bergères in Paris or in the
Sands at Reno. In the richest cities of the world there
are only a few cabarets which can afford to costume a
few dozen dancers with such extravagance. I stood
there thinking that I was seeing what must represent
the total ostrich-plume production of Africa, the total
peacock-feather production of India. Some of the costumes are so heavy that the dancers have to be borne
on floats, where they samba under enormous headdresses and splayed sunbursts of metallic fabrics and
plumes supported by the scaffolding of the float.

At the same time as the parade in the Sambódromo, an equal multitude of people are parading, for
three days and nights, in the Avenida Rio Branco.
The neighborhood clubs, the *blocos*, are parading in

the Avenida 28 de Setembro. Carnaval balls are organized in every building, every hotel and club that has
a hall. Every band that exists in Rio is out playing in
street corners or along the beaches. People who were
not able to costume for an escola dance about these
bands, the poorest slum-dwellers at least costumed
with some dyed chicken feathers.

I could not but wonder at the sheer expenditure
involved, in this Brazil undergoing the worst economic collapse of its history, and reading each day as
I was of the coalition of First World countries spending a billion dollars a day to fight Iraq for control of
Kuwaiti petroleum.

What is distinctive about the Brazilian Carnaval—
say, by contrast with carnival in Venice—is its carnal exuberance. In Venice, the face is masked, the
individual is incognito in a statuesque hierophany.
Here the costume, a sunburst of collars and capes
and a nimbus of arcing plumes, is arrayed as a sort
of shrine around the bared body of the dancer. The
samba, a virile dance, is not a dance of melodic figures of corresponding dancers, but of the legs and
gyrating buttocks, which must be bared. Female nakedness glows in the midst of glorified versions of
culturally feminine or masculine garb; male nakedness glories in the midst of culturally masculine or
feminine garb. The escola Estácio de Sá, whose theme
is "The Dance of the Moon," is gay; 70 percent of its
voluptuous women are transvestites or transsexuals. In
Venice individuals compete for the most extravagant,
original, striking, but also distinctive costume. Here,
everything is communal; each escola parades in *alas*,
troupes of three to four hundred, costumed the same.
Being extravagantly gorgeous is essential to Carnaval,
but so is being part of a collective movement and joy

134

being danced out by hundreds of others in a banked mass. The rows of dancers joyously singing the samba zigzag from one end of the avenue to the other as they advance, each dancer, when he or she reaches the bleachers on either side, throwing out the samba into the crowds, eyes scanning for people intoxicated to dance and sing with. The virtuoso dancers high on the alegorias are not putting on a show to be applauded; they are casting forth spirals of exuberance into the crowds. The parade is not an exhibition of individuals, but a surge of giving, giving carnaval-esque joy to the fireworks-illuminated beauty of the massed people of Rio.

Seeing *sambistas* whose costumes were inspired by those of ancient Egypt, I thought that the processions of pharaohs, emperors, kings were surely never this resplendent. They paraded down the avenues of their capitals in hieratic costume and with ancient crowns and staffs, to fix their iconic figures in the minds of the people as they built triumphal arches and pyra-mids to perpetuate their individuality against the ero-sion of time. Here the art of the most gifted designers of the city who have worked all year on these cos-tumes, drawing inspiration from the arts of all cul-tures and epochs, is but for this night. The dancers whose bodies are glorified by them in the Sambó-dromo stream out into the streets of the city, dancing till exhaustion, abandoning their costumes to the street sweepers before going to their homes.

Around the Sambódromo, there were dances that were more than joyously beautiful.

Anyone who has, himself, scrambled down the Oldu-vai Gorge and tried to make a chipped-stone tool from a pebble found there acquires a personal appreciation

for the skills and perseverance of our "primitive" ancestors. But when he tries to duplicate the hundreds of
minute and regular flakings necessary to make one as
symmetrical as those they made, a symmetry without
any real utilitarian function, he recognizes that a sovereign drive for beauty is as old as humankind. Leopards, jaguars, pumas—splendid in color and form, powerful, graceful, clairvoyant, intelligent—and certainly
not human beings, are the most gorgeous forms of
life. It is not surprising that humans, evolved or de-
volved from other animals, derived their sense of beauty
from other animals. Animals have evolved veritable
organs to be seen:[1] iridescent fins, lizard headcrests, ar-
rays of shimmering plumes, mountain-sheep horns, extravagantly crayoned baboon buttocks—lures for the
appreciative eyes. Every culture in humankind, be-
sides being cultivation of the resources of nature, is a
cultivation by humans of their own nature. Not only
an evolutionary adaption to ecological conditions and social enterprises, but elegance of musculature and contours, colors and garb; choreography of eyes, gestures,
and gait; artistry of caresses, intonations, murmurs,
laughters.

It is one thing to find that the structure of a flower,
its stamen and its protective and insect-supporting petals, is fashioned so as to fit perfectly our notion of
the function of a flower; it is another to find its form
and colors beautiful. We really do not possess a set of concepts that determine our judgment as to what is beautiful; as we go we find that the plastic forms of human bodies, their contours, their surfaces are beautiful
like we come to see the beauty of sand dunes and the geometry and sheen of lilies; we find beauty in somber,
blotched, or veined skin like we had come to see the
beauty of mottled flowers or fallen leaves.

Yet we also have a sense of ideal human beauty.
Ideal human beauty, like the melodic movements of a
herd of zebras in the savannah, the beauty of dragon-
flies crystallizing in sunlight, involves a sense of a
way of life whose felicity is divined. A face can attract us by the fire in its eyes and the vivacity of its
organs, the spiritedness of its substance, the excep-
tional expressiveness of the movements that form and
fade across it; the harmony or vigor of its contours
and tones themselves evoke the benevolence or exuberance of the human habitat. This kind of bodily
beauty makes us thoughtful while dissolving the fix-
ity of our own ethical notions. Certainly the first impression of one who arrives among the Lani of Irian
Jaya or the Ifugao of the Central Luzon Cordillera is
one of physical splendor; it irresistibly contains a
sense of a people who know how to live in the envi-
ronment and who know how to live blessedly. The
more one contemplates their physical poise and grace
in different lights and in different confluences, the
more enigmatic but also the more compelling seems
to be its ethical force. Reading anthropological literature, however, which derives every trait of their mo-
res from ecological and political reasons, reduces their
beauty to anatomical adaptation.

In the crowds and nights of our metropolises and
in our wanderings in towns and fields, we are attracted to the beauty of telephone linemen, nurses,
inner-city schoolteachers, bikers, rice farmers, miners,
street kids in Marrakesh, *capoiera* fighters in Salvador,
women construction workers in Leh. In the beauty of
their bodies we divine so many kinds of talent in living magnanimously. What pleasure we find in discov-
ering them! There are so many who do not know! "It
was Aharon Markus, the pharmacist, who put forth

the supposition that after thousands of years of existence on this earth man was perhaps the only living
creature still imperfectly adapted to his body, of
which he is often ashamed."[2] The ethical sense in us
is elaborated not by concepts and reasons, but by a
sensibility attracted to those who are artists of their
lives.

Like stormy seas and sandstorms in deserts, like
minute and simple forms of life divined beneath the
efforts of vision, and like condors soaring over the
High Andes and leopards passing in ferocious rain-
forest nights, the human body can give rise to the
sense of the sublime. Immanuel Kant would say that
would happen when the scale and pattern of a human
presence exceeds our power to circumscribe it, when
the grandeur of the emperor or the forces of the hero
exceeds our powers of perception and give rise to the
idea of the superhuman or the divine—and this idea
that rises in us radiates in intellectual pleasure.[3] Yet
does not the self-satisfaction in the ideas one forms
diminish the grandeur of the human body and extin-
guish the feeling of sublimity before it? Does not the
sense of the sublime in the sight of a human body
instead empty out the ideas of the superhuman and
the divine?

The material things do not lie bare and naked
before us; they are there by engendering perspectival
deformations, halos, mirages, scattering their colors in
the light and their images on surrounding things.
Human bodies too move in the world engendering
profiles and telescoping images of themselves, casting
shadows, sending off murmurings, echoes, rustlings,
leaving traces and stains. Their freedom is a material
freedom by which they decompose whatever nature
they were given and whatever form culture put on

them, leaving in the streets and the fields the lines
their fingers or feet dance, leaving their warmth in
the hands of others and in the winds, their fluids on
tools and chairs, their visions in the night. Bodies do
not occupy their spot in space and time, filling it to
capacity, such that their beauty would be statuesque.
We do not see bodies whose form and colors are held
by concepts we recognize or reconstitute. We do not
see bodies in their own integrity and inner coherence.
We are struck by the cool eyes of the prince of inner-
city streets, moved by the hand of the old woman
covering the sleep of a child. We are fascinated by
the hands of the Balinese priest drawing invisible
arabesques over flowers and red pigment and water.
Our morning is brightened by a slum-dweller whis-
tling while hauling out garbage. We hear the laughter of Guatemalan campesinos gathered about a jug-
gler, like water cascading in the murmur of the
forest. When we are beguiled by the style with which
the body leaves its tones, glances, shadows, halos, mirages in the world, we see the human body's own
beauty. In the decomposition in our memory, in so
many bodies greeted only with passionate kisses of
parting, we have divined being disseminated a knowing how to live trajectories of time as moments of
grace.

When the scale of a human presence scattered
across vast spaces seems unconceptualizable, as also
the utter simplicity of certain gestures and movements seems undiagrammable, we have before a human body a sense of the sublime. The sublimity of a
body departing into the unmeasurable spaces make
the ideas we form of the superhuman and the divine
seem like second-rate fictions. The sentiment of the
sublime is a disarray in the vision, a turmoil in the

touch that seeks to hold it, a vortex in our sensibility
that makes us ecstatically crave to sacrifice all that we
have and are to it.

Human warmth in the winds, tears and sweat left
in our hands, carnal colors that glow briefly before
the day fades, dreams in the night, patterns decomposing in memory, sending our way momentary illu-
minations: bodies of others that touch us by dismembering. The unconceptualizable forces that break up
the pleasing forms of human beauty and break into
the pain and exultation of the sublime are also delirium and decomposition. Not sublimity in the midst of
abjection: sublime disintegration, sickness, madness.
The exultation before the sublime is also contamina-
tion. Porous bodies exhaling microbes, spasmodically
spreading deliriums, viruses, pollutions, toxins.

Rita Renoir performed in a cabaret in Montparnasse.
What to call this performance? Not dance; it did not
elaborate an artistry of positions and movements. Not
one-woman show; she was not, like Marlene Dietrich
or Madonna, creating a legend or myth of herself. A
female body dismembering and transmigrating. In a
hooded black robe, she emerged; the light glowed
about her hands clasped, hands made for blessing. A
leonine mane hid her face bent over her body in gro-
tesque and obscene nakedness. The shame and malice
of a little girl glowered in a slyly bent torso. Hysteria
raged in a convulsed stomach. Her bared vagina
threatened between powerful thighs. Blood and milk
glistened on breasts and flanks. Laughter hurled pain-
fully against one's ears. Strange garglings and hissings
seduced strangers in the dark. Debauchery splayed her
limbs. Joy strangled her throat. Terrible loneliness
shivered in her. Virility and blood-lust hardened her

legs. The majestic figures of august goddesses miner-
alized her. Longing and interminable waiting ravaged
her strides. Blissful and lethal abandon made her
weightless and floating.

After an hour she would climb over the seats into
the audience inviting people to get on the stage, dis-
robe, and interact with her. Handsome men showed fool-
ish and unwieldy meatiness. Old men revealed torsos
wonderful as those of scorpions. Young men dressed in
jeans and black leather postured their engineered and te-
dious pumpings over limp penises. Elegantly dressed
young women disrobed and showed bodies stilted before hers to the point of ugliness. Stout middle-aged
women glowed with carnal tenderness.

I went weekly for a month, brought friends. Then
I left Paris for the Easter break. When I came back,
the cabaret was closed and I could find out nothing
from shopkeepers in the adjacent buildings. The next
season I returned to Paris, and could learn nothing of
what had become of her. Ten years later, I asked a
friend I had taken to see her, and he told me that he
has never seen any mention of her in the press. I
cannot believe she has secluded herself, like Marlene
Dietrich, with her press reviews and her celebrity. In
Karachi and in Quelzaltenango, on Swayambhunath
and on Komodo island, I looked for her.

A Noite dos Leopardos: for the past four years in the
Teatro Galeria in Botafogo, Eloina dances with her
troupe of bodybuilders. Eloina, with abrupt and precise movements and consummate skill, is supremely,
vaporously, impudently, voluptuously feminine. Like
Nico, who was so beautiful only because her femininity appeared so completely put on, Eloina is able to
separate so completely her vamp, diva, grande dame,

courtesan, czarina, and pop superstar femininity from
femaleness that the wonderful symmetry and propor-
tions of her contours and features seem completely to
obey aesthetic laws. But Eloina also presents the specific beauty of the distinctively female body. Clad, as
it were, only in chains of jewels, the satiny substance
of her full round breasts glow in the light. On spike
heels, her dance does not involve a lot of samba foot-
work. With her full thighs, she gyrates her pelvis in
floating rhythms, and it is as though all the parts of
her gyroscope body—her arms which strike out like
rays from it and bend back elegantly upon it, her
fingers which echo the circular movements, her long
auburn hair reversing its spirals—were assembled to
present the beauty of the pelvic movements. A pelvis
abstracted from any teleological destination to maternity, a pelvis being created just for its beauty. The
idea that Eloina is biologically male floats utterly
detached from what the eyes see.

 Eloina dances with a troupe of a dozen bodybuilders, who walk blasé and impudent on the wild side,
engage coldly and maliciously in knife fights, hurl
themselves nonchalantly at one another in capoeira, a
sort of voluptuous martial art evolved in the bored
black slums of Salvador, prowl, slink, hiss, and leap
on all fours in leopard masks. Their musculature is
completely generic, devoid of the specificities that
individual occupations or sports inevitably inscribe on
a body—not miners' bodies, peasants' bodies, swim-
mers' bodies, power-lifters' bodies, dancers' bodies.
Not personal bodies. Bodies upon which are strapped
a musculature that obeys no finality of development
save that of its own maximum and concordant asser-
tion. Not male-sex bodies, a musculature that like an
accoutrement can be vested upon the invisible theater

of knife fights in the night or the hunt of leopards.
The pleasure of the eye which contemplates the pro-
portions and symmetry of these bodies is inwardly
rent by the spectacle of terrifying feral instincts.

The climactic moment comes when, just before the
final apotheosis, these titans appear in full erection,
flaunting their hard and massive cocks. They do not
gyrate and pump their torsos, and do not dance
lewdly; they advance with movements contrived to
hold the eyes on the sooty glow of their knot-veined
erections. Our eyes are in a state of shock; this position in which they are forced is so contrary to what
they wanted that one protects oneself with a whole
swarming of defensive ideas, Freudian ideas: would
not their wives or girlfriends be completely cheapened
and mortified to see them here? Are not these super-
males in fact sluts, who are not men enough to get
real jobs? What kind of a man would make exhibit-
ing virility his occupation, save those who are in fact
impotent? Are they not in fact narcissists, bodies that,
more than fascinated with their own images, have
projected themselves completely into images of themselves? But it is just through all these questions with
which we undermine the reality of those erections
that we also disconnect in ourselves any libidinal or
emulatory interest in them. No longer male, biological, purposeful whether for copulation or for voluptuous contact, bared of all phallic, political, economic
symbolism, here the erection is asserted for itself, dis-
sipates all finalities we may conceive for it, rises in
savage power for inconceivable intrigues.

One evening I was accosted by a man in rags I assumed needed a handout, and when I handed him a
crumpled bill he gave me a ticket. It was in Manaus;

here, a thousand miles from the sea, the black waters
of the Rio Negro coming from Columbia join the
yellow waters of the Rio Solimões, seven degrees
colder, coming from Peru, to form the Amazon
proper, which is here, at its starting point, eight kilometers wide and three hundred feet deep. Manaus
was the port city of the rubber boom, which abruptly
came to an end in 1912 when the Malaysian rubber
plantations began to flood the world market. I exam-
ined the ticket he had given me; it was for the Teatro
Amazonas, the legendary opera house built during the
rubber boom entirely of stone and marble imported
from Italy and decorated by artisans and painters
from all over Europe; outside the sidewalks leading to
it are of Portuguese marble and the roads of rubber
bricks. It had been seventeen years since an opera
company had come to perform in it.

"Se o espírito de Deus se move en mim, eu canto
commo o Rei David"—"If the spirit of God moves in
me, I will sing like King David"—Edson Cordeiro
rose from below singing. He is very small, with thick
black eyebrows over huge eyes and a great mass of
wild hair well below his shoulders. The voice swelled
with a body, color, range, and expressivity that one
hears and still cannot believe. His second song was
something Yma Sumac used to do, as only she
could—the Peruvian Inca with the five-octave-range
voice. Then he did coloratura arias from Verdi and
Puccini. None of the pinched falsetto of the counter-
tenor in his soprano, rich and vibrant, it filled the
hall with its high-altitude acrobatics. He sang "The
Queen of the Night" from Mozart's *Magic Flute* over
the equally amazing Cássia Eller, a young woman,
hoarsely bawling out Mick Jagger's "I Can't Get No
Satisfaction." He sang flamenco, songs of classical and

contemporary Brazilian composers, blues, religious hymns, Janis Joplin, Prince, and hard rock. There was no intermission. He silenced the applause by immediately beginning to sing again, his voice moving across five octaves, abruptly shifting into another totally different musical universe, each time with purity and gorgeousness of tonal body and passionate interpretation. One would have been enthralled to hear him in any one of these voices the whole evening. The gospel singing brought to the opera house in the midst of this enormous black slum city the fervor of another continent. People dressed in street clothes came through the audience to join him on the stage. The Spirit in the Dark flashed in his eyes and kindled a glossolalia of entranced melodies from him, and jumped across the singers on the stage and sprayed flares across the possessed audience. It turns out, I learned from the paper the next day, that he himself was raised in an Evangelical cult. It was there that he began speaking, and then singing, in tongues. He left home at the age of sixteen and sang in the streets for cruzeiros until two years ago. Now he is twenty-four years old.

His body is very slight, his arms lean, a very adolescent body. He wore soft black leather pants and a soft black leather tank-top, and black boots with high red block heels. Over that he flung on different smock-shirts—a white one, then a transparent one with silver designs, then a red embroidered-silk, Chinese-sleeved one, to finish in a black leather jacket with spiked Kabuki shoulders.

In the flamenco, a duet with Maridol, a professional flamenco singer, his torso arching back to the floor, his arms and fingers were doing even more intricate and sinuous gyrations and arabesques than

hers. In the heavy metal, his body crouched and leapt
with heaving crotch, stopping suddenly, his derrière
vibrating with the drumheads. Physical panic vocal-
ized the Raul Seixas song "Para Nóia." One thought
what a dancer and actor he also is. Except that it is
not that separate thing, dancing, or acting. It is that
the song sings his whole body, is being sung with his
arms, torso, legs, furling, flying, floating in the smoldering or blazing spotlights across the vast spaces and
heights of the stage.

In the concert hall, while one hears the marvelous
beauty of the vocalization, one's eyes stray over the
breasts, the fluid gown, and the thighs of the soprano,
or one's eyes wander over the face, shoulders, and
torso of the baritone and see how handsome a male
body he is. With Edson Cordeiro, so many different
kinds of female voices of so many different kinds of
women are sung with his body that it loses anything
biologically male in it. But it also does not have the
ample voluptuous excess of female breasts, thighs,
that softness of arms and hands that shows through
on singers who look female. There is not a carnal
thickness to the pure melody of his kinesics that
would solicit touch and invite caresses. Everything
that is palpable, opaque tissue, is gone from his body,
which is, I thought, like a mobile Japanese calligra-
phy: an instantaneously made swirl of strokes is so
expressive that you no longer see the hair marks of
the brush and the opaqueness of the ink.

His mouth wide with gleaming teeth is the radiant organ of the song. His eyes flash under those
thick black eyebrows that arc very far back across his
brow. The spotlight beams tangle in the black mane
of his hair. Yet even when doing the most indul-
gently kittenish Janis Joplin song, his face does not

become feminine. It is the only part of him that seemed to me androgenous: the coquettish eyes, the wide sensuous lips on a face whose bony leanness and black cast to the upper lip and chin keep it male.

"Se o espírito de Deus se move en mim, eu canto commo o Rei David," he sang once more from the back heights of the stage as the curtain fell. When he came out to the front edge of the stage to receive the wild ovations of the crowd, I saw how very small he is—he must be barely five feet high. A size not now magnified by glory, for in him there was only a total, innocent joy in song which his radiant face now received swelling back to him from the enraptured crowd.

The transvestite, by outdoing women, doubles up the number with his residual maleness, making of the glamour also an outrage; here the residual maleness itself was transubstantiated into immateriality of song. The beauty was no longer also a way for sexual marginals or members of racial minorities to gain entry into some kind of social acceptance. It was pure, disinterested, absolute. The performance was entitled "Uma Voz"—A Voice—and indeed the wonder was not that a male could sing coloratura soprano arias, but that one voice could have mastered so many different kinds of resplendent lyricism. It was more than stunningly beautiful; it filled the great Opera House, surged across Manaus, sent tidal waves over the Amazon, departed into the jungle and the skies.

One night during Carnaval, there was a Michael Jackson look-alike. Not in the Sambódromo, just having a drink at one of the balls. The same height, same huge eyes, infantile nose, thin lips and gleaming teeth, same cleft chin, same radiant, wild, vulnerable, wanton look. He was also dressed and held his drink like Michael Jackson, and when he danced he danced indefatigably spidery Michael Jackson gambols. One couldn't help staring to try to see some details he had kept for himself: no, none. I realized I was in the presence of an individual in a radically new experience. No doubt there have been people, in the past twenty-five years or so that plastic surgery got going, who, having redone their hair, nose, breasts, like their ideal of beauty, decided to go all the way. A woman who would have redone herself after Elizabeth Taylor or Kim Bassinger could hide it sometimes, with a new hairdo and glasses. But Michael Jackson is a face more stamped in the public mind than any actress ever was, and so distinctive that there just is no way this individual can hide this face he now has—certainly not with shades. He could never go into a room anywhere and not be Michael Jackson. Michael Jackson himself is a product of plastic surgery. This Carioca has wiped away forever his own face to wear the face of a gringo who had wiped away forever his own face.

They say that Michael Jackson's nose is now loosening and beginning to sag. It needs periodic work. I imagined Michael Jackson now redoing everything— dying his skin, having the surgeon build a broad-nostrilled nose, thick lips—and down in Rio this Carioca undergoing the same metamorphosis. I imagined them meeting. They would not be mirror images of one another. Michael Jackson could never be at ease with him. It would be black magic, macumba to him. Already, here in this Carnaval ball full of transvestites, nobody talked or danced with him; their looks glanced off him. By himself, here in Brazil, this Michael Jackson exists, has a space. It would be de-

stroyed if the "real" Michael Jackson not only came
here for a concert, but stayed six months. Clinging to
the beauty he paid for in cruzeiros and pain, this Carioca would have to—would!—create the space for
his single-mindedness, determination, and cool.

I thought that Manila was the ugliest of the sprawling cities of Third World countries whose rural and raw-
material export economies have not ceased to decline
since World War II. Unlike sordid Bangkok sinking into
its muck, stinking Jakarta where but a third of the population has even access to potable water, and the black
hole of despair that is Calcutta, there are not even, in Manila, the tatters of old Asian religions and cultures to
be seen. Its soul, they say wryly, spent four hundred years
in a convent and forty years in Hollywood. Four hundred years of Spanish machismo and forty years of U.S.
marines. The climate is sticky and hot, and the air is poi-
sonous in the streets choked with jeepneys hacking
out black fumes. If you go out you get a headache in
a half hour and will have to change your clothes and
scrub the oily grime off your skin with soap. It is enough
to defeat any quixotic idea of exploring the city one
might have.

It was already 11:30 when I woke, the gut bilious
with another bout of dysentery. The lobby was dark,
the desk clerk asleep on a bench. Outside it was raining listlessly. I walked down streets at random, looking for a bar. Skeletal dogs yapped and howled, picking up from one another, long ahead of me.

Finally I came upon a San Miguel sign; behind
the rusty corrugated metal door a dim light still
glowed. Inside there were some tables and in the
smoky haze a few drunken men bent over them.

A dusty radio coughed out rock'n'roll. On the far wall five women, in dirty dresses, their faces smeared with garish lipstick, looked at me. I sat down in the far corner. A man came to the table. He grinned slyly, showing bad teeth.

"Good evening, sir," he said. "Are you a Yank?"

"A beer," I said.

"Are you alone tonight?" he asked. "Will you have a companion?" He nodded ingratiatingly at the girls at the far wall.

"A beer, just a beer. San Miguel."

"I have very nice girls," he said, "very clean, not like on Del Pilar Street." He leaned over. "No diseases. I have virgin girl for you."

"No," I said as coldly as I could. "I want a beer." He brought the beer. I drank it and signaled for another.

The door pushed open. Outside it was now pouring. I made out in the dark someone dressed in an even more mini miniskirt and even more gaudy lipstick. She was drenched. The bartender yelled in Tagalog at her. She sat at the door. After awhile she came over to my table.

"Do you mind," she said very quietly, "if I sit with you? I don't want anything from you," she said hurriedly, to stop my answer. "I have some money." To prove it, she ordered a beer and paid at once. "I am alone too. It is very late."

I looked at her coarse hands and realized she was a guy. She had a threadbare satin blouse with several buttons missing, and a tangle of costume necklaces over it. On her feet there were muddy sneakers. In her shoulder-length hair she had stuck a now limp red rose. Her nose was bashed in and she had several front teeth missing. I looked down. Then I looked up to smile.

"It is very hot in Manila," she said to my smile. "Excuse me, may I know your name?" "What country are you from?" "How long are you staying in the Philippines?" "Are you having a good time?" Then she stopped.

I said nothing for a long time. I ordered more beers. The bloated feeling in my gut died away. Some of the women along the wall left. I said, "What is your name?"

"It depends on the sun," she said, grinning wide, unconcerned over her missing teeth. "From sunrise to sunset my name is Mario. From sunset to sunrise my name is Maria." She laughed.

She looked at me and said, "Are you sad? Can I sing you a song?" She stood up, tucked in her blouse, tried to untangle some of her necklaces. She bobbed her head, and began to sing "Sad Movies Make Me Cry." She sang into the sputtering of the radio, pulled its canned racket into her own song, she sang louder and louder. She filled the room. The bartender looked vacantly from his chair; the men bent over the tables were beyond hearing. Her eyes opened wide and were lit with flash-fires as she rocked and danced under the bare bulb. Her fingers became soft and her gestures more and more melodramatic. No opera prima donna, no rock superstar, no tragedienne had ever been more splendid, no epic or theatrical or world-historical emotions more overwhelming. When she stopped, she began laughing, spasmodically, wildly, over her song, over herself, a laughter that swept through her whole body and stumbled and fell into itself and pealed out again and again. I was laughing, not sick or drunk. I was shaking with a hilarity that

swept away the yellow bulb, the tables, the room,
that rolled away into the rain.

I looked at the polluted rain muddying my window and thought of the coral seas. I decided to leave
Manila for awhile and go diving in Batangas. I
checked the tourist office and some agents in the city
for information about where to go, where to get diving gear. Her song and her laughter were in the room
when I woke up. I broke out in laughter in the middle of lunch at a restaurant. Four days later I tried
studiously to retrace my steps of that night, but did
not find the San Miguel sign. I tried the next night
again. On the third day I searched for it in the afternoon and found it. I asked the bartender where she
lived. He sent a boy to look for her. They came back
very soon. "Come to Cebu with me!" She looked un-
comprehending. "Come let's look at the fish!" I said,
and waited. Then she did laugh.

I did not rent a boat, even though the beach cot-
tage owner said all the reefs near the shore were
damaged by fishermen dynamiting them to stun the
fish. She had put on a bikini and a red rose in her
hair. The men at the dive shop looked at me and
then down. They asked for my certification card and
would rent only snorkeling gear for her. We carried
the gear to the place where three palm trees shook
their coarse combs over the powdery sand and transparent water. We avoided turning our eyes upward;
the sun was blazing a hole in the sheltering sky. I put
on the scuba gear and sank through into the bolts of
light that flashed across the warm brine toward the
cobalt blue abyss. Below there was surge, and after
equalizing my ear pressure and adjusting my buoyancy compensator to float over the prongs of the coral
banks, I abandoned any effort to direct myself or

swim anywhere. I pulled slices of bread from a plastic bag; damselfish, angelfish, Moorish idols, jackfish, barracudas swarmed about me. I turned over and saw her thrashing above, her laughter cascading through the snorkel in bursts of foam.

I stuck in my bathing suit the corroded half-shell of a pearl oyster and a live decorator crab that had stuck little shells and throbbing anemones all over its legs. I trapped a blowfish in my hands, and knocked it about a few times whenever it started deflating. When my airtank was empty, I swam to the shore. She sat on the sands, surrounded by the sad movies of shells and crabs and jellyfish and laughed and laughed and the waves were laughing against the sands and then turning back to roll their laughter over the Pacific.

V

*****

Pura Dalem

High noon at Kuta on the island of Bali, sea level on the equator: sounds like the coordinates of a target. Across the ocean the sky is blazing. Robots in satellites, hidden in the blue mirage of the sky, are keeping all the movements on the planet under surveillance. After the detonation of a fifteen-megaton atomic bomb on Bikini Atoll, small animals were found to have suffered retinal burns at a distance of 345 miles.

I head for the shelter of a fig tree whose sprawling roots were gripped over a dune as though it were a rock outcropping. White sand, skeletons of coral animals crumbled by the surf, glitter in the scrub hairs of my legs. The tree's branches had sent down aerial roots, some of them plunged poles into the sand, some of them had descended but a foot or so from the limbs and grown fibrous masses of rootlets to absorb the dirty draining of the water from the tree itself during the rainy season, but had died there when the season passed. Insects are shining in the leathery and dusty leaves, all of which are punctured, chewed, spotted from rust or fungus, stunted, or defaced. Torn and yellowed newspapers covered with numbers and disasters stir in hot wind fronts the surf sends over the sand, rush over the dunes and then collapse like tormented evil spirits.

My look ricochets over the scattered palm trees waving their few stiff leaves, drifts on over the dunes,

a radar beam disconnected from the viewing tube in
the control tower. The visions and initiatives that
form in one's life short-circuit in the drifting vapor of
particles; those patterns that endure awhile and which
one calls one's insights, goals, values bleach and flake
off in the sun. The strongest force in the universe is
that which holds the nuclei of atoms together, but it
is not strong enough to resist the attrition of time,
and radioactive isotopes depart, the atom decomposes.

I left the beach and walked back through the deserted lanes of the town. The tourists were still in
their bungalow-hotels and simple inns, *losmans*, lying
on cots under ceiling fans, waiting for the heat to
pass. At the market on the far end of town the produce vendors were gone. Dogs chewed and snarled in
the debris of leaves, husks, and overripe fruits.

I searched for a yard in a back lane where fifteen
years ago, to those who had gone this far from the
multinational corporations and the strategies, hero-
isms, and justifications of the Vietnam War, a taciturn
Balinese woman used to serve "special soup" and
"special omelets." I thought I recognized the yard,
though the grand eclectus parrot and the mangy
black gibbon were gone; their rusting cages held only
chickens. I called. A girl of about twelve came. I
scanned the menu—the usual *soto ayam, gado-gado,
nasi goreng, saté kamping.* "You want mushrooms,"
the girl said. They were black and bitter in the
greasy omelet. I left. I wanted to be on the beach
when the sun squandered the excesses of its glory
before descending into the night.

As I walked I felt the pounding of gongs in the
dust of the main road that led through the town.
Young Balinese women were lining up in pairs; they
wore intricate headdresses of gold and silver filigree

in which pale orchids trembled and sticks of incense smoldered. Men were arriving from the side lanes, armed with kris daggers in scabbards held in the sashes bound about their waists. I recognized dressed in white the court brahminical priests called *pedandas* walking with weightless steps and the village priests called *pemangkus,* old men with warm eyes.

Then bare-chested men advanced in a din of cymbals; among them I saw the female fiend called Rangda, with long cowtail hair, boar-tusk fangs, and long fingernails on her clawlike hands jittery with spells. The dancer behind the Rangda mask was surely already in a trance and was advancing in glides and leaps. A little further was the Barong, a dense-maned beast, its body covered with mirrored dragon scales. Its feet were those of two dancers. Someone once told me that at an ancient date in their history the Balinese managed to ally themselves with the Barong who now protects them from the rages and spells of the Rangda. Men were carrying the instruments of the gamelan: metal timpani played with wood mallets, large hanging gongs, drums, a few stringed instruments, and bamboo flutes. They were pounding out very fast metallic cadences, running in manic rushes into climaxes, reversing, starting again.

The road is completely lined with stalls offering again and again the same stock of color-splashed T-shirts with Kuta Beach as well as Acapulco, Copacabana, Palm Beach, on them; designer jeans faked in Hong Kong; shadow puppets and masks in reduced versions, easier to pack in suitcases; and postcards with photographs of Balinese in traditional costume, cockfights, and the sunset at Kuta. Stalls banked with pirated cassettes relayed from their powerful loudspeakers New York and London disco rhythms from

one end of Kuta to the other; they were not turned
down as the gamelan clanged into them. There were
a few tourists in straw hats looking over the wares or
sucking at a soft drink or a beer; one or another
pulled up a camera and took a few shots of the procession. Nobody followed it. I was not really following
it either; it filled the road, and I did not try to push
my way ahead of it. I too was heading for the beach.

The beach as far as eye could see was now covered with people. Not the hippies of twenty years ago,
but university students in groups, young professionals
in couples, the retired. After the first day the heat
has defeated any idea of going into the nondescript
and traffic-choked town of Denpasar or piling into
cramped open trucks to go into the mountain roads
leading up into the interior of the island. They have
come from thousands of miles to picnic on the beach.
Those who have rented motorcycles have found the
roads full of slow-lumbering herds of the caramel-
colored cattle and the hysterics-prone flocks of ducks
being conducted from the rice terraces by boys waving long canes with bits of tassel on them; they use
their bikes to roar down and back the twenty miles
of the beach, they wade into the surf to wash off the
sand and come up the beach for beer.

They sat in couples and groups. Balinese women
with baskets were laying out cloth hats and bikinis
around them. They were spread prone on the sand
under middle-aged Balinese women fully dressed and
with broad-brimmed hats who were massaging their
backs, rhythmically pressing into the oiled thighs and
buttocks with the heels of their hands. Boys were
circulating with cloth bags from which they furtively
drew fake antique Buddhas, fake kris daggers, and
hashish. In the rondo of the waves advancing and

retreating across the beach, the flotsam and jetsam of
disco and punk phrases rotated out of cassettes.

Ahead of me the Balinese procession made its way
down between the pale, pink, or bronzed bodies; a
few of them sat up, clicked cameras at the folklore,
the travel-brochure natives, the circus Barong and the
Rangda. When the young women with incense smoldering in their headdresses reached the sea, they
turned left and led the others who walked in the
sparkling foam. Expert surfers were speeding on the
gleaming walls of the sea. Bikini-clad couples on
rented motorcycles flared by out of funnels of spraying sand. None of the oiled bodies got up to follow
the procession. I did not follow it either. I turned to
the right and headed to where the beach became
more stony and the dunes were thick with weeds.

I found a hollow between dunes and sat down on
a stretch of sand surrounded by thistles; from here I
could not see anybody, not even on the crests of the
surf below. White conch shells floated on the ripples
that shuddered across the sand. White plovers raced
back and forth across the sheets of wet effervescent
with powdered emeralds and rubies. I heard a cry
tearing at the sky and saw an ashen seabird circling
between the blood-red clouds veined with lightning.
The sun shuddered and fell through the cobalt-blue
sheathing of the abyss. Flash-fires raced down the
shattered water-canyons, spotlighting for an instant
the feathery designs on the shells of blind mollusks.
Indigo starfish climbed slowly downward on branches
of black coral. The tentacles of an octopus etched
with snowflake patterns touched the sands lightly
under a sizzling wall of brine. The sea rolled along
the length of the beach, leaving a long moment of
unresponding silence before repeating its grievance.

PURA DALEM

In that silence I heard the whir of countless fruit bats shooting out of the Goa Lawar caves on the opposite side of Bali. I looked up. The sky was completely black.

When I stood up I could not see the ripples or the weeds of the dunes. No electric music spun in the sands. All the oiled bodies were gone. I heard the long sigh of the undertow; it was the only line in this darkness, and I turned to follow it. The waves washed across my legs hot like black blood.

Then the sands rose under my feet and the sea roared over me. Fish muscles tensed down the length of my spine as my body whipped in the brine. Hundreds of miles beyond, tropical storms raged. The abysses were rent with seisms; molten lava was seething in the faults under seven miles of water and night. The dead roots of a tree reached out for my hand, and I crawled into the boiling sands as the tide raced again and again over me. I opened my eyes and was blinded by the blazing black of the skies.

When I stood up I saw at a great distance stars clustered and trembling. I advanced a long time without getting any closer to them. Then I thought the stars are the lanterns of fishermen in the stillness of the sky looking for lost schools of fish beneath the surface of the storm. Then in the silence that lay heavily after the raving waves sank into the sands, I thought I heard phantom gongs and timpani, as though there was a boat of musicians that was lifted over the sea on a breaker and then walled off from me by another. I stopped, but only heard the sea begin its clamor once again. I walked on. Then it seemed to me that the strange music was ahead of me. I saw fires lurching like torches, then made out a promontory jutting out into the sea. When I got closer, I realized there was a temple. Isolated like this, it must be the Pura Dalem, the Temple of Death.

Along the walls of the temple compound, stone carvings shifted demoniacally. I approached the high gate, open on top like the silhouette of a pagoda sliced down the middle and the two halves pushed apart. On either side stone giants scowled and gripped on maces. People were climbing the steps and entering; they seemed to not see me. I could now hear the shimmering and rushing cadences of the gamelan. Finally I buttoned my shirt and climbed up the half-dozen steps and then down into the temple court.

Adolescent boys and young men sat cross-legged on mats on the ground to the left of the entrance steps; I sat down against the wall behind them. No one glanced at me. Some fifteen feet ahead there was an altar, empty, with tiered roofs of thatching over it; before it two pemangkus in white sarongs and six young women, torsos bound tightly with metallic silk over which their waist-length hair cascaded, were dancing. Their legs were bent and their bodies turned in abrupt reversals; their arms and hands were spread in taut angles as though disjointed from the axis of posture, like the profiles of shadow puppets suspended from canes before a screen. Their fingers fluttered continually; their heads rocked as on rails; their eyes were open very wide and shifted from side to side unblinking. Though their movements were synchronized, they seemed to be unaware of one another. Abruptly the dance stopped and the dancers were surrounded by women who led them to the back of the temple compound.

Women with silver trays of fruits, flowers, and pastries balanced on their heads continued to enter through the gate above me. I watched their brown

feet on the steps open and close the folds of their
sarongs dyed in diagonal patterns of chocolate, ocher,
amber, sienna, and saffron. The pedandas dipped their
fingers in silver dishes and sprinkled perfumed water
over the offerings, then with their thumbs marked a
scarlet smudge on the foreheads of those who had
brought them.

The young men about me had scarlet kamboja
flowers over their right ears and sashes sumptuously
woven with gold threads about their waists. They had
kris daggers in scabbards against their backs. I re-
membered that the blades of kris daggers are made
from metals taken from meteors and laminated by a
now lost art. Those seated about me shifted to make
room for newcomers, murmuring greetings and jokes.
One youth about eighteen with thick-muscled arms
and thighs and flashing eyes from time to time
leaned his hard back against me as though I were
part of the wall.

The gamelan players continually switched tempo
and key, filling the temple court with glimmering
ripples that intersected and in which the people in
the temple rose and receded. The pedandas drifted
back and forth, their fingers drawing complicated
themes in the mists and reverberations. One by one,
women brought their trays of offerings from the altars and now banked them up in the center of the
compound. At the far wall of the compound the Barong was swaying in a sluggish dance. There were no
buildings in the temple compound, and no roof over
it. Curving bamboo poles some twenty feet high had
been planted on the top of the walls of the compound; along them narrow banners were spiraling in
the sea winds. I saw that some stars were now fired
in the storming night above.

Several men got up and seated themselves on the
mats spread over the open area. Pungent smoke
churning out of braziers was thickening in the court-
yard. I sat wedged in the corner by the young man
leaning against me. Through the wall I felt darkness
crowding against the temple compound. The metallic
runs of the gamelan patterns jumped in my brain like
stings. Weariness weighed on me and closed my eyes
and I felt the cold inside me. The crackling phosphorescence behind my closed eyes made me feel dizzy, I
opened my eyes to stabilize myself. For a long time
no one moved across the compound. I watched the
translucent fingers of the pedandas spraying pinches
of incense on the blue flames of the torches.

Suddenly I heard a outcry above; I glared at the
night and saw that on the mats one of the men was
suffering some kind of seizure. He stood stiff on
sprung legs, his arms flailing. Strong young men
jumped up, caught hold of his arms and held him. A
pedanda stood before him, held a handful of smoldering leaves under his face forcing him to draw in the
heavily incensed smoke. He fell limp and began to
sob, then leapt up with rasping shouts. Abruptly a
second man sprang up twisted and shaking. Young
men were at once at his sides and took hold of him
forcibly. But then one after another each of a dozen
men on the mats were overcome by convulsions, ,
springing up or falling forward, flogged with invisible
blows. The metallic cadences of the gamelan raced
between the moans and cries. More young men got
up and struggled to hold the arms and legs of those
in seizure. The pedandas pushed through and were
making signs on their foreheads. I strained forward
and then realized the youth who had been leaning
against me was not there; in a moment I recognized

him, thrown over struggling to hold the clenched fists of a man screaming on the ground.

The gamelan abruptly stopped, and the roar of the surf rolled over the compound. I saw the mask of the Rangda hung on the side of an altar, its eyes opaque in the flickering light of torches. Furious seizures broke out in the mass of men, as though each detonating others. The young men who had been holding the entranced now were themselves collapsing or being flung about by their stiffened and flailing limbs. My head was being pounded by long declamations in gibberish, snortings of wild boars or tigers, gruntings of rodents, shrieks of birds of prey. I recognized the young man who had leaned on me; he was bellowing and choking. I stood up and pushed myself up against the wall. Women and children fled to the far side of the temple compound, where I now saw the Barong stomping its feet, its mirror-scales shooting flares of light.

I tried to jolt my legs into movement to escape through the gate, then fell back: a few feet in front of me a young man had pulled his twisted kris dagger from its scabbard and held it before his chest. With a cry he drove it toward his ribs; the bone seemed to stop it. He now held it upright between his thighs and screaming drove it upwards into his abdomen. Again the point of the dagger seemed stopped by the contorted flesh and did not break through. Now several other men were brandishing daggers; two of them rushed through the gate.

It was not the darkness outside but the white-clad pedandas here that seemed to me some kind of protection. Yet they did not seem to see me, exposed now alone against the wall. And they had themselves released this ferocity which they were not now trying to stop.

These frail old men who stepped into the tangle of armed and entranced bodies seemed to risk nothing. The man in front of me dropped his kris; his body became limp and fell to the ground and lay still. A pedanda picked up the dagger at once and slipped it into the scabbard on the man's back. Another froze, then softened and seated himself looking dazed. The pedandas passed among them touching their foreheads with incantations. The fallen ones muttered or groaned; one or another began to rock, more and more violently, until once again he leapt up or fell forward with tormented outcries. When finally the force seemed completely spent from them, they did not seem to be aware of others who were still being shaken by seizures or shouting.

Five older men had remained seated on the left side of the compound and had seemed impervious to the furies of the night. The pedandas brought those whose violence was spent one by one to these elders. They spoke little, allowing the entranced to have his say. I sensed that they were inducing from the tone, the gestures, and the insistence the meaning of what was being uttered in vocalizations articulated like languages or in animal mutterings. Sometimes the elders seemed to be assenting to what was being brought out or charged. Perhaps troubles known or suspected were being formulated, things which the elders were ready to allow others to bring out into the open. Sometimes the elders conferred summarily with one another, until one seemed to offer a commitment as though to redress the grievance. Sometimes the possessed one was insistent; the elders would repeat the same vocalizations in concession. The gamelan was now silent, and the interviewing was being followed attentively by those who had spoken in inhuman voices and who had already been heard, and by the women and children. Occasionally the elders seemed to be arguing some with the alien voice, as though explaining some situation or justifying some course of action. I saw the young man who had leaned against me, his vociferations being heard out by the elders; eventually he fell silent and sat receiving like a child the ministrations of the pedandas.

Finally there were but four men still in trance. Two were not dressed in temple dress; one man of about forty-five wore a bright red shirt with the name of a disco in California on the back of it. He had glazed eyes as though drunk and yelled querulously. The other, a strong solid-looking man, was dressed derelict and threadbare, and seemed in deep depression. These two now made me think of the patients who rave or moan in the psychiatric and alcoholic wards where I had worked while a college student. Of course, I did not understand the content of what they said. But in the psychiatric wards one thought that a deranged or abnormal mind is not identifiable by the incoherence of the successive parts of its speech or the delusional character of the content of what was said. The loud badgering complaints that went on and on grated on my ears. I suddenly felt intolerably irritated by the pretentious and ignorant old pedandas who were maintaining a sacred solemnity over the ranting of these two malignant fools.

Finally the pedandas administered to these two heavy droughts of the thickly incensed smoke, held them in their caressing hands, and had the Barong led to them. The two men whimpered and buried their heads in his beard as the Barong snapped over them.

The ceremony seemed to have dissipated; the musicians had left the instruments of the gamelan; people stood about conversing in profane tones. No one seemed to be attending to the entranced. I looked at them and they seemed to be feeling embarrassment, perhaps for having departed from the modesty that so governs social interaction among the Balinese. One after another they got up from the mats and slipped outside.

I went out the gate and saw that the community had not left and were gathered at the far end of the promontory. I waited a long time; everyone seemed to be waiting. Behind them the sea rushed upwards and crashed back upon itself. The island of Bali is a volcanic outcropping on the brink of the Wallace Trench which separates Asia from Australia. On the other side of the trench, from Lombok fifteen miles away eastward, no tigers, elephants, or monkeys are to be found; the islands are inhabited by kangaroos, opossums and wombats, casowaries and cockatoos.

I felt awkward standing there looking at the others and stepped back to the side of the temple compound in the darkness for my nerves to stop crackling and for my head to settle. The ground was spongy, and I thought I was standing on graves. The shallow trenches where dead are laid to wait for the families to gather the funds and construct the elaborate ritual vehicle required for cremation. They are buried but temporarily and no headstones mark their graves, but for many, perhaps most, the funds will never be gathered; perhaps after many years their descendants will come to suppose that they have already been cremated. I tried to see if the ground had been broken anywhere, but it was too dark. The earth one treads

on in Bali is compounded with centuries of the de-
composed flesh and crumbled bones of humans. And
of vultures, burrowing rodents, worms, and microbes
that have devoured those corpses and died in turn.
The ashes of the cremated have fallen back upon the
earth and drained into its streams and fields. One
cannot drink the water and eat from the plants without absorbing corpses. Our bodies are the graves of
our ancestors. It was deep-ocean organisms exhaling
gases in living and dying that originally produced this
damp warm atmosphere about the planet in which
we stand upright and with which we speak. All the
air we breathe is the breath of the dead.

Those who had come here to the Pura Dalem this
night had come to make of their bodies the organs with
which the voices of the dead could be heard. Are there
things that are meant to be heard only after they will
have died in their turn? Everything we say responds to
someone who passed on or passed away.

In the wake of the 1965 coup d'état with which
the present military rulers took power in Jakarta, a
hundred thousand alleged or real communists were
hunted down and massacred in the villages in Bali.
In Hiroshima pregnant women have nightmares of
radiation-deformed children. In the white asylums of
Omaha the deranged see aliens.

The social harmony, the restraint of discordant
emotions, the intricate courtesy and ceremoniousness
in social manners in Bali does not derive from religious injunctions or rational social pact; it derives
from the water—the water that must be distributed
to hundreds of autonomous villages, that must be
channeled adequately and proportionately into rice
terraces for each village household. The thousand-
year-old fertility of the rice terraces is that of the

volcanos; volcanos are vast deposits of soluble nutri-
ents. In 1963 Gunung Agung, Bali's most sacred
volcano, mother goddess of the aboriginal Balinese
religion, erupted, laying waste a fifth of the island.
Is there not a trench as deep as the Wallace Trench
in the Balinese consciousness, between the water-
governed ceremonial social existence and the volcanic eruptions, the uncertain and capricious monsoons, the typhoons, heard in trace nights of the
Pura Dalem?

I heard a stirring in the bushes about me. Someone had come to relieve himself. When he turned to
go back I recognized the young man who had leaned
against me. On his eyes, level for a moment with mine,
I saw only the empty darkness. The contact of our bodies was only on mine. Nothing had been communicated. He had not leaned on my white reason; my body
had been part of the wall of the dead. I knew his
name. It was Wayan, or Madé, or Nyoman, or K'tut.
As were the names of these women. The first child in every Balinese home, boy or girl, is named Wayan, the second Madé, the third Nyoman, the fourth K'tut, the
fifth Wayan, and the cycle begins again. At the forty-
day ceremony, the pemangku will write a number of sacred names on leaves, burn them, and whatever might
still be legible in the ashes will be the child's ritual
name. But no one will ever call it this name, and before long the father himself will most often have forgotten what it was. Upon the birth of his own first child,
he will be called Father-of-Wayan, and his own name
will never again be used, and will fade away from
the memory of the village. Perhaps his own children
will not know what it was.

I followed him to the far end of the promontory
where the others were gathered; he joined the young

women who had danced entranced before the altar. They did not glance at me as I stood looking long at their beauty with my indiscreet unseen eyes. They were now smiling and bantering as young men and women like them do in the wake of the tourist procession every afternoon in Kuta. The vaticinations and the rages that had issued from his body had departed absolutely. The lusty vigor of a young male, the flashing eyes of the village cavalier had taken possession of him once more.

What had happened to him he had watched and heard every year since earliest childhood. There had always been the unspoken expectation that one day the possession would come to him. He had felt premonitions, unexplained apparitions in sleep, fevers that arrived and that departed, moments when he realized that chunks were absent from certain hours of the afternoon. He was not, as I had been, afraid that he was losing his sanity; instead, was he not afraid, with a fear far more terrible, of a death that was not his? This fear had not kept him from coming here; it had brought him here.

All that comes from distant white shores, all that is bestial, reptilian in the biles of his body had been brought here, far from the discos and television screens and the white beaches of Kuta, and held in the arms of the Temple of Death. All that which, had there been any communication in the contact of my body with his, my white reason would have inscribed on its surfaces—Oedipus complex, assassination of the father, sedition of youth in every established community, ideological mystifications of neocolonial Third World consumer economies—had been inscribed here in the cosmological orbits.

PURA DALEM

I looked at the gold threads of his sash and the
grinsing—flaming or iridescent—flicker of its colors.
Double *ikat* cloth; the threads of the warp and of the
weave are bound and tie-dyed before weaving, by the
old women of the Bali Aga village of Tenganan,
whose minds can calculate in advance how these
stains of color will intersect on the loom. A sash like
that takes up to five years to weave; he had squandered on it riches he had gained on the beaches of
Kuta selling white men T-shirts and fake Hong Kong
designer jeans, perhaps pimping for them or hustling
them himself. I wondered if in his bank account
forged travelers checks were accumulating to be one
day spent here, in the ostentatious glory with which
the body of his father would be burnt on a cremation
pyre piled high with all his riches, so that the soul of
his father could be reborn, in Bali. I looked at him
and thought, he will not leave this island. His spirit is
already being cremated here, is already being reincar-
nated here.

The gongs and cymbals of the gamelan began to
throb and combine like insects beginning to awaken
in the night. He and the women turned to join the
procession that was forming again. The pedandas and
pemangkus, the children, the women carrying their
consecrated offerings on their heads, the men, the
Barong, and the Rangda advanced down the completely deserted beach. The surf swung the stars stuck
on its walls. Clouds of luminous smoke hung between
streaks of sky. I walked in the foam path spread
along the sea. When the trail of people reached the
level of the main road of Kuta, it turned at a right
angle and entered the town. The long rows of stalls
which lined the descent to the beach were closed and

boarded up. The restaurants in courtyards or open-air
pavilions were full of white men in cutoff jeans,
shirtless or in resort T-shirts, women in bikini halters
and costume jewelry, eating steak and lobster. I did
not see any of them notice the procession as it passed;
surely the gamelan could not be heard through the
white waves of cassette music at the tables where
surfers and sunbathers from the same city in Australia
were getting acquainted.

I felt an abstract hunger and abruptly thought I
should eat. It would take a long time to get served if
I entered one of the restaurants; I went to the far end
of the town, near the market, where there are some
food stalls and had a plate of *nasi goreng.* Down the
lanes, before doorways, sitting on beaches, the villag-
ers still clad in their ceremonial headdresses and flowers were talking animatedly. The assimilation of the
revelations and directions of the Temple of Death was
proceeding. No one greeted me as I passed.

I walked back the length of Kuta to the beach.
The sea was raving and with angry blows drove me
back. On the dunes leaves and empty fruit-juice cartons whipped in the brush and newspapers hissed in
the dark. In the caves of Goa Lawar the great python
stirred, and hundreds of black bats flung themselves
over the jungle with silent sonar screechings. I lay on
the skeletons of the coral flowers which the surf had
crumbled and in which the stars glittered. A cold
wind spread tiny rainbows trapped in bubbles over
the black ocean. Below the storm the stingray shuddered in sheets of sand, its unblinking eyes keeping
watch. Translucent gnatlike damselfish shot themselves free of the egg-mass, and died at once within

the tentacles of an anemone lashing the water. Crimson sea slugs bumped millimeter by millimeter their eyeless itinerary across the prongs of the fire coral. A metal star advanced through the ice clouds in a steady straight line overhead, keeping me under its surveillance.

Khlong Toei

In the Deer Park of Sarnath the Buddha first told, to
five companions, of his dharma. I came to India and
to Sarnath after my second departure from Thailand,
and under its sacred tree, during the afternoon
shower, I spoke with a healer. I stayed with him the
length of the afternoon. The dense crown of the Bô
tree absorbed the warm drizzle; then the sun returned
and vaporized the landscape in white light. He was a
man of some fifty years of age, he wore a *dhoti* and
white mantle, his gestures were infrequent but intricate, and he was of a troubling physical beauty.

People came to him suffering of visible wounds or
the ravages of visible diseases; for these, he told me,
he drew on the Ayurvedic pharmacology of herbal
and mold substances, the knowledge of which he had
received from his father and his father before him.
Men and women came to him also who are not afflicted in some part of their body only, men and
women the core of whose existence is disconnected
from the tasks of society and the appetites of life.
He initiates them into *hathayoga;* it begins with,
and always returns to the *savasana,* the body laid on
the mat with all tension between one muscle set,
one limb, and the next disconnected: the posture
of the corpse. He leads them through an ordered se-
quence of *asanas* in which their bodies learn to maintain for ten minutes, for twenty, for thirty, the equilibrium of a locust, a cobra, an eagle in the sky. Each

time returning to the savasana. He transmits to them
the ancient mantras, sacred sounds which they first
pronounce outwardly, then only inwardly until those
tones without meaning and signaling nothing outside
resonate throughout their bodies only. He prescribes
to them the most rare and precious substances—bits
of gold, of silver, pinches of ground jewels, powdered
crystals from remote Himalayan caves—which they
are to ingest as food for their bodies, in cycles determined by the conjunctures of their astrological charts.

He did not ask for the coordinates for my chart,
and prescribed nothing for me.

"Each one senses the interminable void beyond
toward which the breath of his life is buffeted, and is
afraid," he said. "Men have been able to elaborate a
discourse about the things we successively encounter
around the theme of determinism. This discourse can
draw the lines of a world and locate the locusts, the
cobras, the eagles, and the stars in the darkness ahead
that will put out the light of our life."

"Each one finds himself cast forth and in movement, and turns back to see where this movement
comes from and senses only the empty immensity
before his birth, and is afraid," he said. "Will is what
we call a movement we ourselves launch, when we
turn back and can see nothing of the movement and
path that brought us here. Men have been able to
elaborate a discourse about their appetites and tasks
around the theme of will."

"But the most important events in our lives,"
he said, "would have to be spoken of in a discourse
which we lack. Is a movement auspicious or inau-
spicious? Is an itinerary propitious or ill-omened?
Whether what we encounter is a chance for us is
something that cannot be determined by the discourse

of determinism. Whether what we will is our destiny
or our delusion cannot be decided by the discourse of
will."

"The region found by luck and the path of destiny," he said, "is the high noon world in which we
walk and which is nonetheless dark as the darkness
beyond death and that before birth. In this darkness
we drift as already dead or stillborn. In this region
men hope to encounter healers and guides. The discourse of determinism does not heal and the discourse
of will does not guide."

"An encounter with a guide or a healer," he said,
"itself belongs to chance."

As the sun set and the darkness covered its path
across the skies over Sarnath, we got up to walk,
counterclockwise, around the ruins of the Stupa of
the Buddha.

The night falls very quickly in these latitudes; we
watched the stars being sprinkled overhead. "The
stupa is a mountain," he said. "One does not enter it
as under a roof. It shows you the stars."

"What is called wisdom," he said, "is understanding the patterns and the movements in the most remote distances. It begins when the night covers over
all things close at hand with which practical intelligence concerns itself; the sages were insomniac eyes
open to the stars. It was order, regularity, that the
Egyptians, the Hittites, the Mayas, and the Vedic
seers of the Himalayas saw in the night skies. They
declared that the human soul is destined to the con-
templation of the law that rules eternally in the most
remote heavens. They also thought that the long-
distance vision, and not the myopic practical intelligence that knows expediency, penetrates the most
intimate spaces, those of our own bodies. They saw

writ large in the astral constellations the diagrams of
our own inner constitution; they conceived the saps
that move through our tubes and glands, the appetites
and the tasks that form, to be regulated by cosmic
laws."

"Wisdom is supposed to be very rare," I said.
"Why do most people prefer not to go out into the
night and see how far one can see?"

"Perhaps it is a recent practice that we have not
yet gotten used to," he said.

Something made me remember a conversation
from long ago, with a young student of archeology in
the south of France. "I was told," I said, "that in the
caves of Lascaux the first researchers who studied the
paintings were perplexed by the dichotomy between
the graphic realism of the animals depicted and the
lack of composition. The animals selected and the
numbers seemed to compose neither scenes nor narratives. But they were studying reproductions they had
made of the paintings. On them they saw the layout
and succession of paintings along the walls and corridors of the caves, and saw groupings that were, however, unintelligible. The cave-dwellers had never seen
the walls panoramically; for them the paintings were
visible only successively by torchlight. The Sistine
Chapel depicts the space seen in omnipresent simulta-
neity by the Pantocrator; the paintings in the caves of
Lascaux are in nomadic space."

"In India," he said, "free-standing monumental
buildings do not appear until about two thousand
years ago. The invasions of Alexander in the Indian
subcontinent left the first sculpture representing
the Buddha, in Hellenic robes and gestures, the art
of Gandhara. But Alexander's marches did not leave
free-standing temples in their wake. The oldest

temples in India are decorated caves, and the first
free-standing temples are imitations of caves. In El-
lora the Kailasa temple is a monolith. The mountain
was not cut into stones and then assembled; the stone
of the mountain was cut away to leave the temple."

"I had rediscovered in myself," I said, "what I
thought of as the nomadic kind of vision in the savannah of East Africa. My eyes, repelled by the blazing emptiness of the skies, had been kept on the surface. On the surfaces of the savannah extending on all
sides without paths or landmarks, all one can keep in
sight is a limited segment of the track one has left
behind one."

He looked attentively at me, suddenly more interested when I referred to what I had seen.

"I went to see the Olduvai Gorge," I said, "and the
caves about Lake Bogoria and Lake Turkana where scientists say the first humans took shelter, where their
bones and the bones of the beasts they killed were found.
Only bones left in caves; the surface of the land, the
hills and the plains, bear no more traces of four million years of human lives than it does the paths of the
intercontinental migratory birds. Today Maasai wander the savannah still as the advance of the dry season dries up the ponds, refusing to wound the earth to
establish cultivated fields or even to dig wells."

"India is completely covered with paths," he said.
"And yet there are wanderers."

"Then," I went on, "four thousand years ago, just
north of that trackless savannah, where the Nile de-
scends between the shifting deserts, they built the
pyramids. It was the first dynasties of Memphis and
Thebes that built them. Their sites and sloping trian-
gular sides answered to astronomical geometry. A be-
douin that I met one day said to me, 'Man is afraid

of time, but time is afraid of the pyramids.' I did not understand that, but of all that I heard or read about the pyramids this is the only sentence that has remained with me."

"The pyramids," he said, "locate the stars and the locusts, the vipers, the ibises in the darkness ahead that will have put out the light of our life.

"There were also," he said, "in the shifting wastelands beyond the pyramids, gnostics, who too watched the Egyptian nights. Watched the immense night between and beyond the stars. Their eyes did not see the evidence of sovereign law in the substantial heavenly bodies; they saw that, apart from the infinitesimal girth of the far-scattered stars, almost all is blackness and emptiness."

He moved away a few steps. After awhile he said, "Today advanced telescopes see that the fixed stars, apparently maintaining themselves in the abysses without need of support, are burning themselves out as fast as they can. Electron microscopes see that the cenotaph of our own heart consists, between the infinitesimal cores of material energy in conflagration, of almost all void."

By the time I realized he was gone, the path he had taken was lost in the dark. The rasping of the night insects extended uniformly on all sides. I could barely make out the Stupa of the Buddha. I did not want to tread on the insects in the grass. It occurred to me that millions of them would die this night.

At the gate of the Deer Park I got into a rickshaw to return to the inn, ten kilometers away. The *rickshawwallah* was a man about my age. There was no moon. If one looked forward, one could barely make out things a few paces ahead; if one looked up one could see things millions upon millions of miles away.

I was not alone; I had entrusted myself to this
man for the next hours. Ill-understood, problematical
for us as are the bonds of determinism, freedom, or
chance that connect us to the things about us and the
cosmic spaces in which we are suspended, we are
bound to one another with bonds of trust. Even when,
in the absence of any common language, we can
barely make the other understand our most elementary wants, and certainly cannot understand what he
is thinking. Long ago I had come to think that trust
is the most widely distributed fact in humankind.

The rickshawwallah was silent, bent on making out
the path and the places it forked. Could the Magi have
found the stable where the Jewish Messiah was born
by following the paths of the stars? I carry guidebooks
and maps, but if the map does not make the way
clear to me it is futile to show it to anyone to ask help
in finding the way. If one can first see the layout of
the landscape from above, one locates one's destination and finds one's path to it determined. Like the path
to one's death. People who have never been on an air-
plane, who walk or who pedal rickshaws, cannot read
maps. If one is a mammal or a nomad, one traces a path
in the night or in wilderness, or one follows the traces
of paths others have left in going to their destina-
tions or in going astray. At every bend or fork one has
to choose. As in the path from one's birth.

We arrived at the inn in Varanasi where I was
staying. The rickshawwallah asked where I was going
tomorrow. I had no idea. He said he would take me.
He would be there in the morning. "But maybe I
will not go anywhere," I said. "I will wait for you in
the morning, maybe you will like to go somewhere,"
he said. From my room I looked out the window; I
saw him curled up like an infant in the seat of his

rickshaw. I would have to think of somewhere to go tomorrow. Maybe he would have some idea.

When one goes to sleep one does not depart from the world; one seeks a place in the world where one can be without one's eyes having to scout the environs, without one's hands having to fend off intrusions and disturbances, a place where one can be without going anywhere. The fields and the equipment for a reawakening that will make demands on one anew are confided to the mundane night which harbors them for one. One's sleep rests on a pact of trust made with the surface of things at rest in themselves.

If one were not there. . . . Thinking of what would have happened if one had not been on the job, if one had not been home, gives one a sense of one's significance and responsibility. The world one envisions before one's birth did not require one, was not preparing for one, was not destined for oneself. One is, sometimes, surprised by one's own insight, troubled by one's own impulses, frightened by one's own initiatives. One feels the darkness behind them. And the darkness ahead.

What if you had not been there when those hours or days of my life stretched on, exposed to things and events, to the darkness ahead? What if you had not been born?

"Do you like me?" You approached the bars and with an expressionless face said these words, to me. What kind of question is that? How could the fortuities of nature that produced your body, the Indochinese culture that composed your character, have to answer this morning to my liking? Were you putting yourself under my judgment? Or, more exactly, under

my penchants—for you said your question as soon as
you appeared, without giving me any history to judge.

I did say yes and you said something to the
trustee, no doubt promising something, and he let you
in and locked the door again. "Yesterday," you said,
"a Chinese hung himself in this cell. So nobody
would stay in it." You explained like reading from a
news item in a newspaper. He was a heroin pusher;
they had broken him under the question and he had
named names. When they brought him back he tore
off a leg of his pants and made a noose of it. But you
would stay with me, you said.

You asked who I was. I hesitated. Were you asking what one calls me, where I came from, what I
was doing out there? I never tell the truth about such
things in these latitudes. Being American, one of the
five percent of humanity that has appropriated more
than half of the planet's resources, being a professor
of philosophy, paid to write about values, these are
things that have to be dissimulated if there is to be
any truth between myself and one of you, if there is
to be talk at all. But you knew. The answers I was
forced to give the previous night were overheard and
passed on back here.

We crouched on our haunches against the wall.
Now that you knew my truth would everything you
said be dissimulation?

"How did you learn to speak in my language?" I
asked.

"I am a student," you said.

"Of what?"

"Of . . . political science," you said.

Was I supposed to like political scientists? Were
you studying me here? To whom would you give your
report? I slapped at the flies, rubbed their gore into

the sweat of my leg. You waved at the flies about
you, keeping them moving.

"Are you a Buddhist?" I asked.

"Everybody is a Buddhist here. The king is a
bhikku," you said with finality.

Was I to take this as a piece of your political science? Shoptalk of intellectuals? Monks are called *bhikkus*—beggars. A monk is someone who each morning leaves the wat when the darkness thins enough for
him to see the lines of his hands. He will walk down
the road without searching anything or anyone with his
eyes. If someone comes with food for him, he will
not look at what it is that is offered or at him who offers, for the offering is not made to him in person
but to the *anatta*, the nonself he is supposed to be as-
piring to become. He will therefore not answer, not say,
for example, any thanks. He must eat whatever is
given. King Bhumibol Adulyadej and all the members
of the royal court have shaved their heads and lived
as bhikkus for at least one rainy season. I read that in
some tourist brochure. Were you saying that the king
was a saint? Or that he was a beggar before the generals my country's government seated in power during
the war with Vietnam? Was I to tell you what I know
about factions and intrigues in the embassies, the barracks? Were we to exchange lines from tourist brochures—the exotic Orient, the quaint canals called
khlongs, the land of smiles?

"Where do you come from?" I asked.

"Amper Ganuan."

"Where is that?"

"By Khon Kaen."

"You speak Lao?"

"Yes."

"Are you Laotian?"

"Yes."

"You crossed the Mekong and went to Khon Kaen during the war?"

"The animals died in my village."

"You had relatives in Khon Kaen?"

"No."

"You were in a camp?"

"Yes."

You didn't elaborate. What else should we talk about?

"How long were you in the camp?"

"Two years. A man came from Bangkok and gave my father two hundred baht and took me to work in Bangkok. I worked with a Chinese man."

"What kind of work did you do?"

"I worked in a factory to make clothes."

"How old were you?"

"Eight."

It was still raining. The air was immobile; the rain had not cooled it at all. The wall and my body were slimy. The clouds over Bangkok had been saturated with the exhalations of the fetid canals, the gritty smoke of trucks and three-wheeled *samlors*. The trustee brought the morning's food and handed it through the bars. An aluminum plate of plain rice, and a can of water. I tried to eat the rice with my fingers, of the right hand, for the left is for washing after defecating. One should use the first three fingers only, and the food should touch only to the first joints of the fingers. I was able to lift only big pinches this way, and half of it was dropping back each time onto the plate I held under my chin. I watched your fingers deftly efficient. All the meals of your life had

been prison food. Your stomach was flat and tight,
under your ribs sprung broad.

"How many years did you work in the cotton
mill?"

"One year," you said. "After one year they put me
in a massage house for men."

"Owned also by the Chinese?"

"No. By a colonel."

"A colonel? Did you ever see him?"

"He took me the first night."

"Did you ever see your family again?"

"When I was fourteen."

"Did you stay in Amper Ganuan, with your family?"

"I stole a gun."

"Are there gun shops in Khon Kaen?"

"I went with some boys to wait outside the base at
night. We waited for an officer. The second night he
chose me." You stopped.

I smiled. "Did he like you?"

"When he was asleep I took his money and his
gun. A week later he recognized me in the market
and grabbed me. He told the police I snatched his
gun in the market. They locked me up in Khon
Kaen."

The muscles under the tight skin of your face
locked and shifted as you spoke, to operate your jaw
and not to interpret your words with expressions. I
wanted to disturb this remote anatomical calm.
Shouldn't there be some traces on your body of what
you reported in these phrases of my language? I tried
to think of some question that would trip up your
formulas, and felt weariness and nausea in my gut.

"Do you want opium?" you asked.

"No. But I wish I had some dope."

You got up and went to the bars and called; someone tossed you a cigarette. You sat down and very
attentively emptied out most of the tobacco into a
piece of paper. Then you produced out of your pocket
a small package of dope wrapped in a piece of newspaper and crumbled the leaves and dead flowers off
the stems. You ground it into powder in the palm of
your hand, ground with it some of the tobacco, and
poured the mix back into the empty cigarette tube,
packing it with a matchstick from time to time, with
the patience and deliberation of a jeweler working
with precious stones. Finally you handed it to me and
lit it. Almost at once the sour mass of my body began
to vaporize, and I was overcome with fatigue. I let
my head fall back against the wall. Then I opened
my eyes and said, "It was an American officer."

It seemed to me that I did not sleep at all; I had
only gone through hours in which my mind could not focus on anything. There was from time to time shouting, in the other cells, outside the walls. The horns and
backfiring of the traffic filled these sealed walls with ha-
rassment and pointless agitation. I opened my eyes a little and saw your hand lying at your side, and saw you
were missing a finger of the right hand. I turned away
and closed my eyes. Then you were touching me,
you had another cigarette. I drew on it and felt nauseous and drowsy and unable to stop the viscous images in my head. During the war the Pathet Lao told
young peasants to chop off their trigger fingers to get re-
jected from induction in the army.

I tried to jolt my consciousness and formulate some
question. You opened the eyes on your smooth face;
they were opaque. It seemed to me you could never have
spoken to me. Speaking, about political and economic
forces, about causes, about the conditions for and the

forms of militancy, is what I have done for years, in
buildings on the other side of the planet. I made out
records, marked cards, assigned or refused credits for
diplomas for hundreds of names I have forgotten. I
had traveled to Indochina and would return to diagram political and economic maps on blackboards;
my diagrams about the ways commitments take form
in the map of psychic forces look scientific. One day,
in front of a desk, I will imagine you and write one
set of sentences and then, later, another. I learned,
in classrooms years ago, how to select nouns and
verbs grammatically marked as concrete from those
marked as abstract. The one set short-circuits to an
ideal order of universality and law; the other shunts
to what reverberates in the nervous system as reality.
The proper blend of the two types of words gives an
effect of consistency. A little chemical substance can
produce a few moments of metaphysics in the brain.
It was for a transgression of the rules of the market, done solely out of private interest, that I was
put there, and the plastic cards I had at my disposal
would release me from your presence. It seemed to
me strange that you knew some words from my
kind of talk.

The trustee came with aluminum plates of plain
rice. I saw that outside it was dark. Mosquitos had
drifted in. One does not see them; one hears their
whine against one's ears. The bare bulbs remained
illuminated. It was now impossible to sleep. I felt too
nauseous to smoke any more. The talk in the other
cells was louder, querulous. There was shouting back
and forth; sometimes you shouted back something.
Twice I looked at you and asked if you were all right.
You said yes, as though you had no understanding of
the menace the hours themselves might be. What is

there in the years of your life I could ask you about?
"Do you have brothers and sisters?"
"Seven."
"Are you the youngest or the oldest?"
"Middle."
"What do your brothers and sisters do?"
"I don't know."
The muddy dawn came, the guards turned off the
lights and opened the monkey cages so that we could
go to the toilet. Before the sink I studied my yellow-
ing jaundiced abdomen. The mosquitos had left hard
brown welts. You came back with Puangkaeow. She
was young, her blouse was missing half its buttons.
Her black eyes slid in their fluids like primitive marine animals turned unstably on me. She spoke with
you and from time to time turned impassively to me.
When the trustee brought the aluminum plates of
rice, she brought out of a pink plastic bag lumps of
colored glutinous rice wrapped in shreds of banana
leaves. I watched her fingers, as though animated
with programming of their own, break and stir the
food. I went through my repertoire of stock expressions in Thai with her. She, very engrossed in this,
pointed to the plate, the rice, the bag, the walls, and
pronounced for me the Thai words, then pointed to
the parts of my body and pronounced the Thai words.
They did not stick to my mind, and when we tried
it again I could not supply the sounds. She kept a
hand in yours, or a leg in contact with yours. I used
the chain she wore about her neck as an alibi to
touch her; I lifted it and saw it held a coarse blue
sapphire. I looked at it closely, and at the slight
movements in her throat as she breathed and swal-
lowed. She pulled forth the chain you wore; it had a
black star sapphire on it. Then she ran her fingers

lightly over the corridors of the intricate tattoo in blue lines that covered your chest and began to read the ciphers, pronouncing them one by one.

"What did that mean?" I asked.

You did not know how to translate it for me. Perhaps for you they were mantras, and not statements.

"It is for protection," you said.

Her thin fingers opened the paper with the dope, and long and attentively picked out twigs and seeds, leaving the dry leaves and flowers, which she then ground into powder in the palm of one hand. She has, I thought, the fingers of a poisoner. The acrid smoke filled my mouth, and the cramps in my gut subsided, not as though through healing, but as though my glands and organs, bilious and jaundiced, were drifting away into the rain and the slime.

You and she stood to dance. You held your legs hard and bent, as though ready to leap or strike. Your hands and arms formed tense angular patterns and marked rhythms in the horns and backfiring of the traffic outside to which you danced. Your dance was not the courtly Siamese diagrams I had watched in the gardens of tourist restaurants, but dreams of bandit princes in the Shan mountains. The sapphires which you had stolen from the miners of Chantaburi were hurled in your movements. Jewels such as these are not made to be set in the crowns of those who sit on thrones; they are the riches of nomads in the steppes or in the Himalayan passes. They are not cut to hold and distribute facets of light; uncut and unpolished, they gleam about the arm that throws its projectiles, about the limbs that race through the night casting torches into settlements. Flares of light flashed and disappeared in the night of your eyes. Was something being narrated in the sprung

diagrams of your bodies? Was this dance, these stolen
jewels, these drugs your truth?

My eyes scummed over. You and Puangkaeow
stopped. You laid some papers on the floor and had
me lie flat and spread your thin sarong over my head
and arms. The nausea of the bile in me I had choked
with the smoke dulled me, disintegrated the effort of
my mind to focus. I woke grappling at your sleeve,
which you pulled back violently. I started to get up,
then fell back, wrenching away from myself.

When they turned off the lights we had to rise.
They opened the gates and we went to the toilet,
and then they brought the aluminum plates of rice
and the cans of water. Bobot came back into the cage
with you. He is nineteen. He speaks no English. But
every muscle, every surface on him speaks. He holds
his huge eyes fixed on me; the words shaped by his
positions and gestures tell of his childhood on the
other side of the Mekong, of the bombings, of the
fires, of movements by night in serpent-infested jungle. I understood everything. What a transparency the
bare muscles and angles of his lean body are! If I do
not yet know what he did between the ages of seven
and fifteen, and the succession of events that brought
him last year into this cage, that is only a question of
the time it will take to tell it, on the agitated fine
musculature of his face and lean hands not veiled by
the duplicity of signs.

And you—how much you speak now, how easily,
about your existence! I say little, and you do not in-
terrogate me about myself. Out of discretion, out of
slyness? Lying back, you pick up thread after thread
of your life without incitement from me. I hear you
answering questions I did not dare ask. Why is there
no wariness in you? Militant, bandit—all that you

say to me, a stranger, is risky for you. It's a prostitute's compulsion, I thought. They always talked.
About the first orgasm, the first time for money.
About the pimps, the way one gets tied up. About the
good ones, the insatiable ones, the rich ones, the de-
praved ones. Even more easily than they slip off their
clothes, they tell it. As though that's their real job,
delegated representatives of the lower depths, making
their reports, their confessions. As though they realize
that is what you want, that there is not enough in
the coupling of lubricated organs to hold your interest, to make you overcome your spite at not having
been able to do that for yourself or for free. The possible but unverifiable truth of what they say is only
there to beguile.

I tried to shake together the double track running
in my mind, looked into your eyes, and started seeing
the lines of your body doubled with equivocation. Its
virile shape seemed something made by a mold. Was
it youth alone that maintained this shape, despite the
lack of solid food, the lack of exercise in these cages
for how many years now? I tried to imagine how you
would look if middle age made you fat and bald; I
tried to imagine you then, as now, bent over me arranging a bed of paper and a sarong for me. There
was something missing in this maternal image. Your
finger—in what male contest did you lose it?

The trustee came to lock the cages for the night.
Puangkaeow went to him and spoke with him; she
and Bobot stayed. They prepared another cigarette;
the sour smoke churned in my wet body and I felt
not the torpor of sleep coming on but only the ebbing
away of my forces. I lay back on the paper laid on
the wet floor. She bent over me and began to massage my feet and legs, applying hard thumb points of

pressure to stop and release the blood in the veins.
Then she worked on my arms. When she turned to
my chest, I took her in my hands and pulled her
down on me. I was imprisoned under her. I closed my
eyes under her damp hair and lay in a black pool of
hatred of you.

The next day the vice-consul came, with an inter-
preter. He gave me a list of lawyers; the first on the
list, he said, was intelligent enough to have graduated
fifth in her class at Thammassat Law School five
years ago. She is married to an inspector of police. He
bailed me out to the hospital. Two days later I was
sentenced by the court—to pay a fine of two hundred
baht, and be expelled from the country within
twenty-four hours. I saw the little man with the
tense, twisted ears who had planted the dope on me
standing at the back of the courtroom; my lawyer said
he would receive half the fine. The lawyer accompanied me back to the monkey cages of Khlong Toei to
pay the bail; I also bought ten cartons of cigarettes. I
stood there, with her, to insist that the guards really
pass them through the bars. They saw me. They will
think now, I thought hopelessly, that that American
was a good guy. They will generalize. But we had all
been there because of the Americans.

The hill tribes of the Himalayan foothills, living
off slash-and-burn agriculture in the jungle, had always used some of the opium that grows wild there,
as Chinese old people used opium, as the aged in Mo-
rocco smoke kif. During the war the CIA contacted
the remnants of the Kuomintang army which had
been in the Golden Triangle in southern Burma and
northern Thailand since the flight of Chiang Kai-shek
to Taiwan, and contracted them to supply opium to
finance recruitment of saboteurs among the monta-

gnards of Vietnam and Laos. The generals of Saigon skimmed off rich profits from this trade, notably Air Marshal Nguyen Cao Key, who controlled the flights. When, in the final days of the war, the American troops were being shipped home, returning to the jobless slums, heroin addiction among them was a matter of serious concern in Washington. It was impossible to intercept heroin in the innumerable lines of shipment; the only alternative was to try to cut off the production at the sources. The Nixon government then arranged a large grant of money and equipment to Thailand to wipe out production of heroin in the Golden Triangle. The funds were transferred to the military junta installed in Bangkok, among whom were those whose attention was devoted less to government or even to defense than to the exploitation of the resources of the country and to swelling bank accounts abroad which they could join when Thailand too fell to advancing Viet armies. The antinarcotics investment then made it necessary to arrest a certain quantity of peddlers and smugglers. Rather than send the ill-paid troops into the mountain strongholds of the heroin warlords, they had the police in Bangkok employ informers, addicts themselves, to entrap novice smugglers. The Thais are a proud people, the only country in south Asia never to have been subjugated by European imperialism; they resent being treated by foreigners as a land of addicts responsible for the drugging of youth in the slums of the richest nation on the planet. To make this point they arrest a certain number of Americans. And I, good guy passing through Khlong Toei, was dissembling what I am with my cigarettes of tobacco.

The flight was at 11:00, Aeroflot, plane change in
Moscow. In Paris my old friend Franck took me to
his bank and took out three thousand francs for an
airticket. I wired the lawyer five hundred to begin to
work for your release. My conviction and expulsion
order written in my passport is in Thai; no one but
Thais can read it. I went to the embassy and reported
it stolen, got a new passport, and boarded the plane
for New York. I wired Franck back the six hundred
dollars he had advanced me. But at the end of the
month when I got my bank statement, I found that
the exchange rate had fluctuated, and that when they
converted the sum I had sent, Franck had received
some four hundred francs less than what he had
passed on to me. I wrote him an embarrassed explanation, of the delay the bank operation had required
and of how it was impossible for my bank to wire
him the money already converted into French francs.
"Let us be grateful," he wrote me back, "that the
system does not work as well as we had feared."

When my leave began the following winter, I
went to Papua New Guinea and Java. When my Indonesian visa ran out, I still had three weeks before I
had to return. Looking at brochures at a travel
agency, I saw that one could now enter Thailand
without a visa if one had a paid airticket for departure within fourteen days. I bought a ticket from
Jakarta to Bangkok, continuing on to India fourteen
days later. On the plane from Jakarta to Bangkok I
had several drinks, and the turmoil below the level of
awareness emptied my mind. I got off the plane and
got in the line marked Immigration. When the officer
handed me back my passport with its stamp, and I
took a step beyond, I abruptly realized that that was

it: they did not have all their police and immigration
lists computerized; I was admitted. I repeated to myself, happily, Franck's words: "Let us be grateful that
the system does not work as well as we had feared."

I had now two weeks to find you. I contacted the
lawyer. She had received my wires. She thought Puangkaeow might still be in Bangkok. I got a roomboy
from my hotel to go learn all the lawyer knew, and
then go search for Puangkaeow. I waited in the hotel.
The lawyer had said that if I accompanied the roomboy people would probably tell nothing. After three days
he learned that Puangkaeow was working in a textile
factory in Thon Buri. The following day I went with the
roomboy and the lawyer to the factory. We waited
for the end of the work shift. The foreman brought
her. She greeted us timidly and formally. We sat down
on stools at a soup stall in an alley near the khlong.
The alley reverberated with the never-ending racket of
motorcycles and samlors coughing their cheap fuel
mixes into the air over which heavy clouds hovered.
The lawyer perhaps thought that going to a restaurant would intimidate her, and while I thought of first
going somewhere quiet, as one would in my country,
I was full of nervous impatience to hear her tell where
I could find you.

She said you had leaped off a roof to kill yourself.
Soon after I had left, on the night of the first full
moon. The roof of a two-story building. Her fingers
rested by her side; her face was still, her eyes vacant.
There are no buildings high enough, as in the cities
of my country, for people of Thon Buri to dash themselves into instantaneous death. You had leaped from
the roof of two-story building. It had taken three days
for you to die.

She had no idea where to find Bobot.

VI

*****

Coals of Fire

You lay sprawled out in the heat. Your face lay like
mud over your clotted mind. You had no idea how to
shape your lips. You couldn't think of what you had
wanted them to murmur. The darkness weighed so
heavily on your eyes you did not know if they were
open or closed. You did not know if you were still
breathing. A rain of pungent night passed over you;
you were drenched in her hair. You could not push
from your brain the muddled sleep that had saturated
the mass of your body like the clouds and fog of the
monsoon that would lie over the delta for months.
You thought you would be washed by the flooding
river into the silt-filled bay. You heard her muffled
voice saying "You are dead." She groped for your
hand, as though to go with you. So that you would
not be alone in your dying, so that someone, anyone,
would be there.

Had you then come to the far side of the planet,
to this tropical mire, in order to die and in order to
find her? No, you had had no idea. You had had no
destination in your goings and stoppings; you had not
directed your existence to any termination, to this
endless Orient in which you were drifting. It had
been only some accident of the chemistry in your
glands, some chance microbe, that had let this mortal
torpor into your veins and nerves. It had been only
some accident of chemistry that one day had brought
the one spermatozoon out of thousands that died in

the ovum which then began to divide into more cells. Before the slow fever of your existence got contrived in those cells there had only been the endless black tunnel of time in which no cosmic scheme, no moral imperative, had planned for you. She shook your legs angrily and said, "You are a corpse."

The desk clerk studied what you had scribbled into the ledger and scowled. "You must answer every question," he ordered. "What is your religion? How many nights are you staying in Dhaka? What is your next destination?"

"Well, I don't know how long I am staying or where I am going from here," you said, suddenly full of weary irritation. What is there to see in this country?

"You have to answer all the questions," the clerk repeated in a loud voice. "This ledger is inspected by the police."

You took the ledger. After "Religion" you wrote *unknown*. After "Coming from" you wrote *Rangoon*. "Going to"—you could not think of the name of another town in the country. You scribbled *moon*. You rotated the ledger and pushed it to him.

He studied what you had written, his face tense and officious. "Where is this—Moon?" he asked you severely.

It was two o'clock in the morning and hot and you had stupidly not bought a bottle of anything in the duty-free of the airport at Rangoon. There had been no alcohol available on the Biman plane. This is a Muslim country.

"Where is your next destination?" he demanded.

You grabbed the ledger and wrote *MOON* in capital letters two lines high.

"What are you doing?" he shouted. "Why are you scribbling all over my ledger?"

"Just give me a bed for the night," you said.

"You get out of here!" he barked. "Guard! Guard!"

"Look, I'm sorry."

Four security guards closed in on you. You had three heavy suitcases, full of books. You began pulling one a few feet, then pulling the next, making a show of being exhausted. A white man came into the hotel; you asked him where there was another hotel.

"The only other one is the Intercontinental," he said, in a German accent.

You asked the doorman for the name of another hotel. He did not answer. The guards stood against you, ordered you to move away. You said, "I am out of your hotel. This is a public street."

They pushed you on. A cab pulled up, let out a passenger, but refused to take you. A middle-aged man in a threadbare business suit looked at you wrathfully and said, "Why are you making trouble?"

"Oh mind your own business," you mumbled.

"What?" he hissed. "What did you say? Why are you abusing people who are doing their jobs? There are jails in this country for the likes of you!"

You looked at his bony frame and felt like picking him up, shaking fists and all, and dropping him on the other side of the street. "Is this your hotel?" you muttered. "You don't know what you are talking about. I didn't do anything to you."

He stiffened and grimaced. "I spit on you!" he shot out. "Do you think you can buy up people and push them around like suitcases?" His speech was studiously Oxbridge accented. "This is our city and our street. Do you people think that everybody here is just waiting for you to show up? Just waiting here to give you everything they have for the privilege of having your fat bodies in their beds?" He was swallowing syllables in seizures of rage. A crowd was gathering.

A man in dirty shorts poked at you, "You want a taxi." He piled up your suitcases in the back of an unmarked car, said, "Give me ten takas."

You handed him five.

"Ten takas!" he shouted, blocking your way.

You pushed him aside, pulled open the door, got in front. The driver looked at him, did not start the car.

"Five takas more!" the man outside demanded.

You pulled out the five takas and handed it to him.

"Take me to a hotel," you said to the man in the car. "A cheap hotel."

He worked at getting the car started, drove through a maze of filthy alleys, pulled up in front of the locked gates of a guesthouse, shouted something. The guard looked at you, said the guesthouse was full. Another, a third, a fourth, all full. The driver pulled in front of a narrow alley. Several old men gathered around the car.

"Is there a room for the night?" you asked.

One went off, shouted, came back. They pulled out the suitcases, piled them on a rickshaw. The driver said the taxi fare was a hundred takas. You gave him fifty and told the rickshaw puller to move on to where the room was. He stood immobile looking at you. You handed another twenty takas to the driver, then thirty, then walked alongside the rickshaw into the alley.

Three old men that had been sprawled against one another in a doorway got up and grabbed your

suitcases, reeling under their weight, then hoisted
them on their heads. You climbed four flights of
stairs behind them. A shirtless young man with bad
teeth said there was a room without fan for fifty
takas, a room with fan for seventy-five. You took the
room for seventy-five; there was a cot and one small
window, high and whitewashed over. You handed the
men who had brought the suitcases five takas each;
they demanded ten. You pushed them out. A scrawny
child came with a spraygun, for the mosquitos, he
said, and sprayed stinking insecticide over the room
and the cot; roaches staggered out onto the floor, fell
on their backs, lay there jerking their wire legs. You
went to the hall, splashed water over your face out of
a pail in the toilet.

When you got back to the room, a bent old man
with thick stubble on his jaw was there. He said, "I
will bring you a companion, how much you pay?"

You said, "I don't want anyone."

He said, "Very nice," twisting his decrepit torso
into obscene wiggles, puckering his mouth and wet-
ting his lips. "Very young girl, very clean."

He pulled up to you, took hold of your hand. You
pushed him out and shut the door. The latch was
loose in the doorframe. You turned on the switch for
the overhead fan, and its big paddles turned; you took
off all your clothes and lay on the cot. The doorknob
rattled, the door pushed open; the old man was there,
behind him you saw a tiny woman in the dark. A
strong odor of rancid perfume enveloped her. She
grinned, showing a space between her front teeth.
You said no, and pushed the door shut on them. You
laid down again.

The old man pushed the door in and said, "You do
not like, sahib? Only one hundred takas, the whole

night, she do everything. I bring another, what kind
you like? you like English girl, sahib?"

You pushed him roughly out of the room and
down the corridor and down the stairs. You pushed
your suitcases under the cot and shut off the light.
You woke in the dark, and turned on the light. It had
seemed to you that the cot had collapsed, the building
sunk slowly and leveled out like a house built by
children out of sand on a beach when the tide begins
to turn and the sheets of water rise higher and
higher.

Your limbs heavy and limp lay immobile like the
body parts of another, of anyone at all. You felt the
rain of her hair pass over your face, then falling in
streams over your throat. You felt her warm breath
over your ribs. One March day when you were a
child you had crouched in high grass by the river and
the wind had passed through the branches of the wil-
low trees and filled them with tassels of small flowers
over which the yellow pollen drizzled, and under the
dead grass mushrooms and small violets on wiry
stems emerged from the wet earth. She stirred over
you and moved your arms, laying them aside with
your hands upturned. "Is it day yet?" you asked. "It is
always night," she said. She kissed you on the mouth
with a terrible urgency. After a few minutes you realized she was sleeping. Her breath was slow but its
wind filled the whole building. You could no longer
distinguish the long drone of the waves of the river
from the sound of her breathing. All tension, all will,
had gone out of the substance of her body; a cold fear
passed across your nerves and you thought she was
dead. But it seemed to you that the rain of hair over
your eyes and the mouth wet on your chest were

alive, like the river outside that had wandered two
thousand miles from the eternal glaciers weeping under the Himalayan sun.

After you had shaved and dressed, you put little pad-
locks on each of your suitcases, put your traveler's
checks and passport and airticket into your camera
bag, and went out. The young man with bad teeth
was dozing in a chair. You asked a rickshawwallah to
take you to a hotel. He pedaled you to a colonial
building with thick stucco walls set behind a big
muddy yard where piles of broken plaster wall lay
under barren ugly trees full of crows, repeating in the
same tone their stupid comment about anything. A
fat woman wearing a half-dozen copper bangles on
her wrists and a half-dozen tarnished chains with
crosses and medallions over her breasts greeted you
expansively. She said she was a Christian too, an Ar-
menian. The room was huge, low-ceilinged, and
musty. The air conditioner rattled and dripped water
onto a black stain on the floor. The roomboy in livery
brought you gin and a bottle of tonic water in a silver
bucket of ice. There was a tasseled velvet bedspread
on the big square bed with its sagging springs, a
pointlessly complicated wicker armchair, a lamp with
draped lampshade, a table by the window with a
worn linen tablecloth and a linen napkin rolled in a
silver napkin ring. How much more opulent all this is
than the multinational-corporation comforts of the
Intercontinental. You sensed the hands of liveried
servants, called by a touch on the call buzzer, hand-
ing messages and bringing tea to the wives of imperial officers and agents of London shipping compa-
nies, who had all vanished. You had never seen one
of them in London. The opulence lay now in the

dark-curtained dampness of this room like the veils
and five-thousand-year-old flowers from the banks of
the Nile in the tombs of the pharaohs of Memphis
and Thebes. You pulled out a book, but the lines
glued up before your eyes. You could think of nothing whatever to do outside in the city. Your nervous
system was made of straw. Your skin was made of
cardboard. You left the room and walked the streets.
The stalls of all the vendors had been boarded up and
all the lights put out.

"As you know," the old man explained in an imper-
sonal tinny voice as though reciting a report to some
U.N. commission he had memorized, "the partition of
the Indian subcontinent, at the end of the days of the
British Raj, was followed by widespread communal
riots and massive exoduses of minority peoples from
the new nations of the Indian Union and Muslim
Pakistan. The civil administration, police, and transportation and communication systems in East Bengal,
now East Pakistan, had been intentionally kept in the
hands of Hindus by the British imperial rule; most of
these now left for India. The new government in
Dhaka appealed for qualified personnel from Muslim
India to immigrate to East Pakistan. A very large
majority of those who immigrated came from the
Indian state of Bihar, immediately adjacent to Bengal
to the northwest, and one of the most overpopulated
regions of the Ganges plain. During the twenty-four
years of East Pakistan, these people staffed the administration, police, and postal and transportation
systems, as well as factories, but retained their Urdu
language and ethnic identity, frequently returned to
Bihar to visit their relatives, and used their savings to
buy property in Bihar for investment and eventual

retirement. By 1970 the Bengali national independence movement had implanted itself deeply in the highly articulate masses of Bengal; in June of 1970 the Mukti Bahini openly called for armed insurrection against Pakistan, that is, against the military government of Islamabad and economic exploitation for the profit of the Punjab. The repression that followed was of unparalleled savagery, and by June 1971 the U.N. refugee commission reported that there were ten million refugees in India, principally in Indian West Bengal. General Yahyah Khan sent in more and more units of the Pakistan regular army from the Punjab; the Urdu-speaking Biharis in the civil administration and police opposed any dismemberment of Pakistan. Finally, in December of 1971, Indira Gandhi's government sent in the Indian army massively, which in ten days overran East Pakistan. The units of the Pakistan army, encircled, surrendered and were held as prisoners of war. Fearing massacres by way of reprisals against the Biharis in administrative posts, the International Red Cross intervened to set up sixty-six camps in which some eight hundred thousand of the civil personnel were isolated with their families for their own protection. The Geneva Camp in Dhaka was the largest of these."

The old man stopped to pour more tea for you. It was thick and sugary.

"By mid-1972," he resumed, "the ninety thousand troops of the Pakistan regular army were repatriated by train across India to Pakistan. Some of the civil administrators, accused of crimes against humanity, were held for often summary judicial proceedings by the authorities of the new nation of Bangladesh. In accordance with the terms of the 1973 Simla-Delhi agreement, the Red Cross administered a questionnaire to the

Biharis in the camps, requiring of them that they specify their option—for Bangladesh, Indian, or Pakistani citizenship—and specify whether it was unquali-
fied or with second options. Those in the camps were
in terror of Bengali vengeance, and, being trained administrators, railroad personnel, factory workers, and so
on, expected that Pakistan would be forced to recognize their loyalty to Islamabad during the civil war by
finding positions for them in Pakistan. They reasoned
that the new civilian government of Zulfikar Ali Bhutto
in Islamabad would have to purge the administration
of military appointees. The majority of the Biharis in the
Red Cross camps in Bangladesh declared themselves—
irrevocably—for repatriation to Pakistan. When they
did so, the government in Dhaka proceeded to seize their
properties and holdings in Bangladesh and distribute
them to the heroes of the Mukti Bahini. At the same
time, the Indian government passed a measure to se-
quester the properties in Bihar owned by these people
who had declared themselves irrevocably committed
to Pakistani nationality. But their repatriation was not
to come about. General Yahyah Khan was overthrown, held in detention, and the new Pakistani Pres-
ident Bhutto was fully occupied, not only with trying
to maintain in a ruined economy the first civilian government Pakistan had known since 1958, but also
with containing the separatist movements now viru-
lent in Sind, Baluchistan, and the Northwest Frontier.
After arranging the transfer of 125,000 of those in the
camps, the government in Islamabad procrastinated
on one motive and then another, in fact not being willing to accept the immigration of eight hundred thousand now destitute persons with no family, ethnic, or lin-
guistic ties to Pakistan."

209

The old man stopped and was silent. His eyes drifted, his hands groped at the pile of papers on the table. Then he went on, in the same flat voice. "In the ten years that have elapsed, some 125,000 more from the camps, those who had connections in the Punjab or had managed to conceal funds somewhere, had bought themselves visas and passage to Pakistan. Some had been able to cross the border into India to find refuge with relatives in Bihar. A smaller number had managed to lose themselves in Bangladesh, doing the most shunned kinds of brute labor for half the wages of Bengali lumpen proletarians. In 1977 the International Red Cross terminated its dole of seven pounds of wheat monthly per adult, withdrew its administration of the camps, having failed in six years of negotiations to find a political solution, and having failed to induce the Biharis to relinquish their demand for repatriation to Pakistan. It turned over its records to the Pakistan embassy. Those in the camps were now dependent on relief from private organizations, mainly Oxfam and the Mennonite Church. In 1978 the government in Islamabad by ordinance rescinded citizenship of those in the camps in Bangladesh."

The old man stopped. He did not look at you. You said nothing. You got up to leave.

You had not been able to locate any tourist office or even map of Dhaka. *Dhak* means "hidden" in Bengali. The monuments you had noticed seemed to be either administrative buildings built by the Raj or small brick mosques. This must be another of the cities of the Indian subcontinent where shantytowns spread like an epidemic around a port built by the

British East India Company. The street walls are covered with webs and webs of a writing you did not understand—probably the names of the leaders and the slogans of a couple of dozen political parties, impotent anyhow under the present military rule of General Ziaur Rahman. The rain trees are enormous, arching maternally over the roads, with fine-cut fernlike leaves over which black mynahs jump, shouting *Joy!* Against the whitewashed walls of a mosque frangipani trees brush their yellow-throated white flowers like kisses. Kites chatter and soar like huge swallows over the piles of plantains and mangos in the market. Your eyes no longer stop on the dogs and cats that turn with the enfeebled and hopeless movements of the children of the city. The gleaming metallic crows hop over walls and roofs of shanties like robins in the white suburbs where you came from. Fruit bats, glossy and thick-furred as raccoons, hang in clusters on the low street lights and look at you with big clairvoyant eyes; when the lights are turned on they unhook and depart noiselessly into the red splendor of the tropical twilight. Butterflies crowd and dance over piles of decaying refuse, as innocent of fear as ten thousand years ago when no human tracks were yet seen on the new alluvial islands the Ganges spreads further each monsoon into the sea.

The washroom cleaner finally ventured to ask you to visit his home. You took a bus four miles out of the city. You walked over the walls of fields filled with water and sky on which a foam of rice spread sprays of clear yellow beads. Rows of coconut trees strode with you down canal walls; their stiff plumes shimmering in the heat waves were held in precise designs on the unwrinkled sheets of water below. You walked

211

COALS OF FIRE

a long time over rice pond walls; it seemed to you
that you were walking over floating planks of mud,
that you were far out at sea, over whose still infinity
masses of gilded seaweed drifted. Sonar Bangla,
golden Bengal. At regular intervals small domed
mosques rolled like buoys. Finally you reached his
island. His house had yellow-clay walls, smoothed by
his hands—a piece of sculpture to be unveiled still
covered with palm-leaf thatching. His wife offered
you the baby to kiss and her eyelids lowered shyly
over her lustrous eyes as you drew near. He invited
you inside; there were jute sacks for sleeping, nothing
else, not even spare garments hanging anywhere. He
brought the jute sacks outside and you sat down in
the shade of his mango tree. He tied a dead palm leaf
into a loop, put it about his ankles, then hoisted himself barefoot up the coarse scales of the trunk of the
coconut tree; from the top he detached a green coconut and dropped it down. When he descended he
offered you its milk. What could you offer him? You
would have wanted to photograph his teen-age wife,
but must not; you photographed the baby clinging to
his bare chest. He told you he was feeding his baby
Nestlé's baby food so that it would grow up strong
like an American. He does not know that commercial
baby food does not have the immunizing agents natural in mother's milk. He buys powdered baby food,
which has to be mixed with water, which he can only
draw from the rice-field canal. You made a mental
note to buy some bangles the next day as a gift to his
wife.

Around you were the bales of jute and bags of sugar waiting to be loaded, jute for bags for transport-
ing commodities to consumers in cities on other

continents, sugar for their coffee and ice cream. The long murmur of the waves ran along the rafts of bales and bags that would soon be afloat. Her blood in drops pushed through silk veins sending their vibrations into your muscles, like the muffled tappings of prisoners by night on thick walls. You felt their tropical heat beating against the membranes of her lips. You felt the wet waves of her breath across your face, whispering "Your penis is as cold as death. You did not cry when your mother pushed you out of her womb."

You had walked back from the waterfront as the black sky turned purple. The dogs lay dropped on the cool muddy streets; you stepped between them and cast no shadow over them. When you reached your hotel you lay on the big square bed, closed your eyes, and listened to the immense silence. You got up and climbed the stairs to the roof. Crimson fumes spread upward from the rim of the earth; the sulphurous sun rose like a monstrous bubble out of the muck and mists and turned white. It filled the city with such an excess of light that you rose floating and your gaze could no longer locate the rain tree that sprayed across the window of your room.

The fact is that the government of no nation state is willing to cede to the Biharis any of the space of the planet it possesses for them to live. The Bangladesh government wants no part of these allies of the defeated oppressor. Pakistan does not want these rootless people in her territory. India is unwilling to allow these propertyless expatriates to come to Bihar. They have appealed to their fellow Muslims in the rich nations of Saudi Arabia, Kuwait, and Libya, offering to do any menial labor in those deserts—to deaf ears.

The International Red Cross has withdrawn, no U.N. commission holds meetings to discuss their lot; no government's embassy is arranging the purchase of arms for them; no reporters in quest of news come among them. The solution the populations and the governments of the planet have in effect decided for them is: Die. The community of nations does not want to take the initiative to execute them. It wants them to die off, by themselves. That is all it awaits of them, all that it has made possible for them.

The lanes of the Geneva Camp within the city limits of Dhaka, where twenty-two thousand people are interned in a former football field, are full of children. They are in no way educated, neither in the conceptual stock of culture, nor in any kind of useful skill. There are no doctors; epidemics regularly spread across the camp. But, in the darkness of the hovels, the emaciated adults grapple at one another, breeding and refusing the death sentence humanity has put on their race.

One has to die. To die is something one has to do, oneself. Even in the complete absence of any knowledge, skill, reasons, implements, physical strength, to do anything. It is true that dying is something that happens to an organism—a car crushes one's vital organs, microbes lay waste to them, one's physical processes of renewal progressively fail. One can let oneself be killed—be another accomplice of the homicide the forces of nature wreak ceaselessly on our kind of existence. But that too is something one does.

How can one do something when one has neither implements nor any materials nor knowledge nor strength with which to do this, save one's own still awake vitality? This thing one has to do—to die— one can nonetheless do with others. The others that

stand close by are as remote from one's life as the
death that is at any moment imminent. One dies in
the arms of others, by the hands of others. In the
quiet of white hospitals, the doctors, one's family and
friends who are also one's doctors, tell one the time
has come, have told each one who got born how it
has to be done. When they lay in one's arms and held
one collapsed in voluptuous abandon, were they not
making seductive the abysses of extinction? When the
other that held one is also lost, still others will, beyond appeal, judge how it was done. Humankind is
silent about the Biharis, waiting. All the others, the
men and women organized into the community of
nations which have taken possession of the earth, demand of the Biharis that they do this—die.

Humankind that has propagated its life and its
will without reasons and doomed uncounted races of
animal life to extinction, is satisfied when it can find
reasons to obliterate a segment of its own inconceiv-
ably excessive numbers. The imputation of guilt is
the mental operation required for always ad hoc poli-
cies. The Biharis were accomplices of the terrible
butchers of the Punjab; at least three million died in
the struggle for national liberation in 1971. Those
who wordlessly condemn the Biharis to die—the rest
of mankind—are not willing to execute them after a
juridical procedure conducted before an international
tribunal; one would also have to put on the stand the
rulers in Washington who supplied the arms of
Yahyah Khan, and the revolutionaries of Beijing who
piously declared neutrality before the war of national
liberation in Bengal, and the boards of directors of
multinational corporations that have secured half of
the planet's resources in the white hands of the nation that contains 5 percent of humanity.

The Biharis were preparing to die. They were preparing it carefully, patiently, daily, as they lay unsleeping on the ground of the camps. It was something they were to do to themselves and to their wives, their parents, their children; they were spending those long unemployed hours and days hardening the resolve, pushing its way through every resistance, every weak nerve. After their attempted "Long March" out of the camps across India to Pakistan was halted on the Bangladesh border in August 1979 by the arrayed armies of Bangladesh and India, they declared that beginning March 2, 1980, they would put an end in immolation to their existence. They would issue out of the camps, converge before the futurist Government Hall and High Court buildings designed by the architect Louis Khan, and pour kerosene over themselves and die in the flames. They were going to do that, die on their own imperative, separating with their hands pouring sheets of kerosene the imperative of this dying from the sentence of humankind, leaving all the guilt there in the blazing skies that spread over the community of nations.

You woke under the crests of the wind the ceiling fan was spreading over your body. You pulled open the drapes; the sun had already set. Bulbul birds, breasts red as the sky, were fluttering in the leaves of the rain tree. On the table you have books about other places, other enterprises, the destiny of Greece and the technological future, full of the constructions of reason. There is no reason to be reading them in this dank hotel room rather than elsewhere. Each day you have been assigning tasks to yourself, consulting the hotel staff whose incessant talk abruptly halts when you appear, who mobilize for whatever you come up with—mending a torn pants pocket, locating a mailing envelope in the market to mail some books now read and weighing down the suitcases. Inquiring from one window to another in the post office, you let yourself be led about by some mendicant who zealously reviews the different postal regulations with you, prolonging the time, displaying his knowledge and his usefulness to you, indulging his pride. Why don't you take the train to Chittagong and go walk the sands that extend unspoiled a hundred miles along the Bay of Bengal? Why don't you go see the villages of the hill tribes along the Assamese border? Why don't you go to India, visit the tiger sanctuary in Nagaland, the Black Pagoda covered with erotic carvings in Konarak? Why are you spending another night here? What is there to understand in this Devanagari script that webs all over the walls and doors and windows? A political, or religious, or ethnic march that will bring the army with *lathis?* A rock hurled at your head in a dark lane?

A tropical virus on the moist surfaces you touch enters your porous organism every day. The eggs of the female mosquito can mature only if she has absorbed blood. When the mosquito punctures the skin, its saliva is injected, which stops blood-clotting, and with it often the single-celled plasmodia. These migrate to the liver, where they feed and grow. Each one divides into forty thousand merozoites, which live in red blood cells, where they grow again, and each one splits into twelve more. Each time they divide another stage of malarial fever comes upon their host. The larvae of hookworms live in the soil; they are capable of boring through the skin of the feet. They migrate to the stomach walls, where they remain hooked and drawing in blood, injecting chemicals to

217

COALS OF FIRE

prevent clotting. Schistosomiasis, or bilharzia, lives in
the blood vessels of the intestines or bladder. Eggs
pass out with the urine, miracidia hatch out in slow-
moving water and enter the bodies of water snails of
the species *Oncomelania quadrasi*. They metamor-
phose twice into fork-tailed cercaria, which shimmy
through the water and bore into the legs of anyone
splashed from a puddle in which they exist. Your
mind each day laid out projects, plans, reconstructed a
personage with a task and a role, as though this mental activity brought to light an individual destiny
plotted out by nature and in the interstices of the
social order. In this place, where you stayed for no
reason, you could die, your destiny fade off into nothingness, like the narcotic light effects beamed out
over accidents. Was your need for the heat of love or
libidinal agitation intended, called for, required? Was
it not a chemical accident that the fluids in your
mother's womb washed one sperm out of thousands
that die there to attach itself to the ovum that then
began to swell and divide? Behind the accident, the
utter nothingness of you, lay the nature and the cosmos in which who could then, who could now, dis-
cern any plot, design, requirement for you?

You touched the buzzer and ordered dinner. The
roomboy brought mango chutney, curried pomfret,
saffron rice, some plantains, a pastry, and tea, and
laid them out with white-gloved hands.

She cried out her pain, her legs shook spasmodically
as though sectioned from the motor axes of her body.
Her belly twisted and recoiled. Her eyes glared into
you with voracious application, as though all the electromagnetic fields of her brain had suddenly contracted into this voracity, as though she would never

again be able to desire anything else on the planet or
in the heavens. Her hands kneaded your body; her
torso shifted and sank its weight into you, her elbows,
her ankles, her toes, her shoulders, her wrists, her
vertebrae, her ligaments, her tendons, her ribs, her
belly, her sphincter, her labia, her vulva, her eyelids,
her earlobes, her nostrils, her pores, her saliva, her
sweat, her odors, her milk, her fluids, her fermentations, the valves of her heart, her sobs, her vociferations, her stridencies, her throat, her

At the gate of the hotel there were several rickshaws
waiting. The men crowded about you, talked in
hushed tones. "Very nice girl, sahib! Just sit down
here, sahib, I will take you! English girl, sahib!"

Whatever price they tell you, for whatever it is,
you will offer a third of what they said. You will go
up five takas. Then you will say *no* and turn away.
Then you will offer five takas more. You will say "I
don't want" and walk away. Several times you will
insist, "One hundred takas, everything included? No
extras? No tips? No transportation charge?"

You climbed into a rickshaw. The old man was
wearing only dirty shorts; you watched the vertebrae
shifting down his back as his feet on the pedals pushed
the chain that turned the axle. When you passed a
light you saw the bones of this thighs and legs line
up and fold as he transferred his weight from one side
to the other. You felt the shifting of his bare heels
on the pedals, felt the shifting of the bone under his
weight being communicated down the chain and the
axle, through the creaking frame of the rickshaw, to the
seat under you. From time to time he got off and
pulled the rickshaw up a rise in the road, his feet pushing against the muck. His asthmatic breathing in the

malodorous air rasped your ears. He stopped the rickshaw at a boatlike rusted American car from twenty years
ago; three men were inside. There was a rapid exchange in Bengali; then you were asked to get into
the car. You said you would wait here. They urged you
to get in, said it is only a short ride, ten minutes; you
will choose for yourself which one you like. Here they
cannot bring anyone, there are police. They want to
take you where in Dhaka there are no police. They
opened the door, the rickshawwallah urged you to come
down, you got into the car. After ten minutes the car
stopped and you paid, and they wanted you to get into
another rickshaw. He pedaled you down some lanes.
On the way word was passed on to another rickshawwallah. You waited in the dark lane of drifting scabby
dogs. You heard coughing in the shanties. Another rickshaw was pulled up, with the rainguard sheet of oilcloth dropped over it. You were asked to get in and
choose. Inside you could not make them out in the dark.
They clung to you, you tried to feel their caresses,
your lips were dry and your shirt stuck to your chest.
The rickshawwallahs urged you with hushed jabber-
ings. You said one only; you said, for no reason, the one
on your left. At once the other climbed out, and the rickshawwallah closed the oilcloth rainguard and the rickshaw lurched on a very long time. When it stopped and
you got out, you made out the wharf; you heard the
long murmur of the waves running between the piles
of the docks. Another man appeared and led you into a
warehouse through corridors between bales of jute
and sacks of sugar piled high on wooden flats. He spread
some dirty cotton sheets over straw and left you with
the candle. She was very young, was wearing a cotton
sari with short blouse. She had a dozen copper and
plastic bangles on her arms. There was a copper cobra

bracelet around her left ankle. Her body was enveloped in a heavy odor of musk and scorched amber.

After the communal riots that followed the partition of the Punjab, the government in Delhi commissioned the architect Le Corbusier to design a new administrative capital for the Indian part of the Punjab, to design not only the public buildings, but the urban layout, the residential dwellings, even the furniture. The architect was not to incorporate traditional Indian motifs; Nehru said the new city of Chandigarh would be turned wholly to the future. In 1965 General Ayub Khan, who had seized power in Pakistan, commissioned the American architect Louis Khan to design new public buildings for Dhaka. Made of bricks and with techniques available locally, laid out with the sun and the winds in mind, the American-designed administrative capital was to be not only beautiful and monumental, but the model for construction throughout Muslim Bengal. You were told at the desk it was some seven miles across the city from the hotel. You took a rickshaw. Every few blocks there was a huge square pit filled with stagnant water choked with the masses of water hyacinths, their inedible thick leaves bright green, their flowers an unhealthy pale violet, thick with flies. Some of the pits were being dug; men and women were spading out the thick clay into wooden forms for bricks, which they put out to bake in the blazing sun. The city is made of these bricks, roofed over with sheets of corrugated metal, palm-leaf thatching, or sheets of plastic or tarpaper. The rain is continually wearing down the bricks, draining in yellow rivulets back into the pits. In the bands of earth about the houses vegetables are grown; along the railroad tracks, the canals, there were pineapple thickets, the knobs of cabbages, cucumber

vines. There were clumps of banana trees, like sprawling mutations of the grass, betel, coconut, and oil palms,
great mango trees and papaya trees that were just
stems with a few leaves spread over heavy hanging
fruits. Along the road vendors sold strong tea, milk, and
fruit and sugarcane juices in unbaked clay cups which
were smashed on the ground when emptied. The rains
will reduce them to mud, and with time level the
mounds. There were piles of decaying vegetable scraps
and husks, vibrating with hornets and butterflies. Beggars, children, dogs furrowed over the mounds; men
scraped up the decayed muck into sacks to spread between their plantings. Girls wandered down the road collecting in baskets cow and ox dung, which would be
slapped on the walls of the houses in round cakes to dry;
they would be burnt for cooking. Under trees kerosene cans were being cut apart and pounded into pots,
lanterns, dippers, spoons; old truck tires were being
cut into sandals; bottles were being refilled and caps
bent again over them. Small children were scaveng-
ing for cigarette butts; they will be opened and new cigarettes rolled around the wads of wet tobacco with
strips of newspaper covered with Devanagari script.

You asked the rickshawwallah to stop; you got out
and sat down at a stand and ordered some tea. The
tea was thick as soup and sugary; you poured con-
densed milk into it from a can. A rancid stench hung
in the air. You walked down a lane; the stench thick-
ened. At a turn of the lane there was an area the size
of a football field choked with hovels covered with
palm leaves and rotting rags. There was a trench
around it. You saw children with bloated bellies
squatting on the banks of the trench, over yellow
muddy puddles of fecal matter. They saw your camera, bunched up with intertwined arms and shouted

to be photographed. They urged you to come to a
plank laid across the trench. You crossed the moat of
muck and stench. The lanes were narrow and slippery
between cells made of palm leaves, rags, papers hung
on bamboo poles, in which people lay or sat crouched
up. There were rusty metal containers with herbs
growing, fastened on the palm- or banana-leaf roofs.
Some young men surrounded you and smiled and led
you by the hand further into the camp. People were
cooking rice in clay pots over cow-dung fires smoldering in depressions in the ground. They stared out as
though you were some kind of apparition. The sun
was pounding on your head; you looked up and saw it
sweeping its fires across all this tinder. There was a
middle-aged woman with hair caked with cow dung.
There were lepers, but they did not poke out the
stumps of their hands to you for alms. There was a
child that grinned a mirthless grin and uttered phrase
after phrase with hoarse gasps between them. A man
completely naked followed you and broke out in sobs,
then stopped, then sobbed again. There were no rickshaws. None of the deranged ones showed any sign of
hurling himself against the reason in your head.
There were eyes that did not see; there were goiters
hanging in loose boils on throats. There were no
shops, no piles of objects in the open hovels.

The young men led you to a shanty over which
there was a flag flying, with a crescent moon of Is-
lam. Two men were brought who spoke English. One
had a scraggly white beard and tortoise-shell eye-
glasses; without asking you who you were or telling
you who he was, he at once recounted before you
the history of the Biharis in Bangladesh. He told it
clearly and chronologically, taking pains with the

dates. He showed you letters typed on limp paper, appeals drawn up to the United Nations, to private international organizations, to the rulers of Pakistan, Saudi Arabia, Kuwait, to the Sheik at Mecca. You tired at once trying to read this documentary prose, full of relative clauses. Is it a certain code that finally one day makes the contact, unleashes an action in some cubicle in the partitioned and coded surface of the planet? He continued his explanations in precise, elegant British, that of a barrister in the courts of an empire that can no longer be located. The other one that spoke English was a youth wearing a dhoti, who told you his name was Abdul and that he was eighteen. What else could he say to identify himself— where he had been, what he had done? He had a broad face with warm clear eyes, and very even teeth. His chest was covered with a mat of black hair. He followed you outside. Then he told you, in carefully spaced words as though explaining to a child, that he would immolate himself within two weeks in front of the High Court in Dhaka. He looked one after another at the young men crowded against him, arms around one another's shoulders or hands clasped at their sides. They will bare their chests and pour kerosene on their bodies. Their flesh will blister and boil, after an hour their bones will smoulder, and will stink. The young men led you by the hand through all the lanes of the camp. They urged you to take photographs. But wherever you turned your camera, the children crowded in to fill the view, with laughing faces. When you turned the camera up to record the hovels, they leapt high before it, shouting and laughing. The sun was setting; it was soon too dark to record anything on your 100-ASA film. When the roll

was used up, you did not put in a new roll; you
pointed the camera at the clumps of children and
clicked the shutter again and again.

Her left hand had deep in her palm lines you do not
know how to read. Her fingers were small and black.
She wore a copper ring with a big stone of red glass
in which the flame of the candle flashed. Her laughter was coming in spasms from her loins tight about
you, shaking her soft belly, her navel was laughing,
you felt the laughter down her thighs loose against
your arms. Her violet lips tightened and shivered
with her laughter. You felt her blood churning and
foaming. You lay your face over her belly and turned
it over and over in the sweat crackling with flakes of
candlelight. Her laughter poured in tears over your
thighs. The black bales of jute slid aside as on dollies;
an immense tide of milky blue poured over you; you
felt yourself rising weightless and drifting over the
high branches of the raintrees, the blue surging up
against the icy foam of the clouds.

You walked out of the gates of the hotel past all the
rickshawwallahs and did not look at them. Several of
them continued to follow you along the road, tapping
their bells on the posts of their rickshaws, a harsh metallic entreaty that you tried to flee by weaving between the stalls of the market. You walked under the
great maternal rain trees. You stopped and asked for
some tea from a vendor. You sat down on the great bulging root of an ancient, demented banyan tree; all its old
limbs had aerial roots descending to the ground like
crutches. Some of the crutches had stopped halfway
down, divided into thick masses of fibrous roots, dead
now as the fibers of a broom, covered with the dust of

the sky. As you drank your tea you looked into the
thick succulent blades of some yuccalike plant, and at
the stalk that lay curving on the ground, ending in a scarlet knob of scales, like an ear of corn, out of which
here and there filmy blood-red orchids spread. You asked
the vendor what one calls this flower in Bengali. She
did not know. On the numbered shelves of a library in
your country, there are books with tables in which its genus and species are given, along with a diagram of
its leaves, its tuberous or fibrous root system, its flowers, its seeds. It is a mistake to think that the birds are
leaping about at random. If ten species of birds are
on the tree overhead, one species is picking on the
buds, another on the seeds, another drawing nectar from
the flowers, another feeding on one kind of insect, another waiting to dart out into passing swarms of gnats,
another looking at vegetable debris on the ground, another waiting for a dog or a rat to die. One must not
let one's brain be misled by the flux of the senses, by the
Maya. There is a strict code governing the number of
rickshawwallahs in front of the hotel. When you climb
into a rickshaw and let yourself get pedaled into a
dark lane, the puller will not pick up a stone and smash
your skull. Where you say he will go; he will give
you your change for the agreed fare. The beggar
child will follow you, but stop as soon as you give
him a coin of five paise. There are codes governing
every stand where plantains are laid out, where different kinds of rice are sold. Along all these walls over
which the Devanagari graffiti scribble their abstractions, their slogans and buzzwords for dozens of impotent political parties, there are codes squaring off every cell of the space, every unit of the time. On Friday
afternoons the market is as deserted as a shopping
mall on Sunday mornings in the white suburbs. When

the temperature rises five degrees, when you descended three hundred feet from the plains of Pagan
to sea level here on the deltas of the Ganges and the
Brahmaputra, the chemical solutions in your brain required time to find the new formula. It was through
their temporarily ill-dissolved residues that your brain
was recording blurred and dim impressions. The targeting pod known as Pave Tack mounted in an F111
fighter bomber flying six hundred miles an hour at an
altitude of less than five hundred feet is capable of locating a single building with radar and then with infrared cameras and releasing a bomb guided by a heat
sensor; the targeting pod is made from nickel- and ti-
tanium-based memory alloys, iron and boron amor-
phous-alloy cores, silicon steel, aluminum-oxide Lanx-
ide composites, and currently costs fifteen million
dollars. The community of nations has occupied every
square meter of the surface of the planet, and coded all
the flowers, the seeds, the birds, the metals, and the
salts. The worldwide sale of weapons yields now the
equivalent of the total annual production of the poorest 20 percent of laborers. The total annual productive labor of one out of five humans goes into amassing the
weapons to exterminate the others.

You waited in the warehouse between the piles of
jute bales and sugar bags. They brought her. They
moved off, and you knew they would be waiting
about the doors of the warehouse. There were unsleeping men everywhere on the docks. You buried
your face in her hair, pressed her tight against your
stomach, ran your hands along her vertebrae and ribs
and shoulders, under her arms and between her
thighs. You wanted to enter her entirely, to make her

your grave. You wanted your eyes to see only her
darkness, your surfaces to feel only the coursing of
her blood and fermentations. You glared with hatred
at her eyes in which you could see only the flash-fires
in her inner darkness ignited by the candle on the
floor. "Tell me your name," you demanded. She
pressed her lips against your mouth, held your head
tightly. You forced yourself back, then pressed your
lips against her throat. Why, you thought, do each
time I have to tell some loiterer always waiting in
front of my hotel, then take this rickshaw, pay it, pay
this taxi, take this other rickshaw, pay it, come each
time through different streets, wait for them to bring
you here? Who are all these men that own you? You
looked fiercely at her and felt fear crackling in all the
bales of jute and sacks of sugar. "Tell me something,
anything, about you, where you live, what you do.
Tell me where you were born; tell me who your father is." You saw the rims of her eyes wet with black
tears. "Why can't you come to my hotel? I am paying
for my room. I can bring in anyone whenever I like."
She put her mouth against yours, snuffed out your
words with her tongue, clasped your fingers. "Tell me
your name," you demanded. She drifted back from
you. You pulled up on your elbows and repeated,
"Tell me your name." She rose and you looked up
her smooth black skin blacker than the night. You
grabbed her ankles, kissed the copper cobra bracelet
around her left ankle. You buried your head in her
loins and mumbled the words into her womb: "Tell
me your name." She bent over you and whispered in
your ear, "Gita." "Gita," you said, and you thought
Gita is the name of a dancer in a Hindu temple, she
is not a Hindu, those men are Biharis, Gita is the

name of a temple prostitute. "Ask me something about me!" you shouted. You dropped back on the ground and lay there. "Your name is not Gita," you said. "Gita what else? What name did your mother give you?" She pressed her mouth softly against yours, and you felt her hair shimmering over your chest like fire.

Accompaniment

We awaken not because we are driven, by inner hungers and thirsts, to seek out substances we lack in the outlying world; it is our energies generated during sleep that awaken us, seeking to be discharged. Our eyelids lift, our gaze departs in the morning light. It sinks into the surfaces of illuminated things, absorbed by them, leaving them where they are. Our breath exhales our longings and euphorias into the winds. In labor, in play, in walking, in laughter, we leave our energies in the things massed along the way. The landscape absorbs our sweat, tears, reflections, and shadow.

In seeing, in hearing, in touching, in walking, our life finds support and sustenance in the light that buoys it up and carries it into the distances, in the rumble of nature which carries outward the crest of sound our breath utters, in the substances that guide our touch, and in the ground that rises up in the things and maintains them in their places and us in our movements unto them. In every movement that reaches toward exterior things which we look upon as moveable, manipulatable, useable, consumable, we sense the contingency of the reality that supports and sustains us. Whatever is at a distance is a possibility until we take hold of it, but when we reach for it, it may take hold of us. Might not what lures us ensnare us, might not the strings we pull enmesh us, might not the path before us end in an impasse? The abyss

lurks behind the connections of things and beneath
the paths where they beckon.

In fatigue one senses the fields of the world no
longer supporting one's position, no longer sustaining
one's movements and one's enterprises. In boredom
the planes of the landscape lose their significance, the
force of their presence; the paths become equivalent,
lose their urgencies. One feels the emptiness that is in
each thing, the abyss over which the paths scurry.
Fatigue and boredom give way to apprehensiveness.
In the emptiness of days, in insomniac nights, anxiety
clenches the heart.

In this finding oneself adrift, supported by nothing, nothing to hold onto, one's life that still exists
cleaves to itself. One comes to feel the heat and the
pulse of one's own potential for existence. One senses
in oneself powers to feel things no one has yet felt, to
perceive corners of the landscape hidden from others,
to form thoughts no one has ever thought and fashion
things no one else can make, to pour one's kisses and
caresses on minute and on grand things and on bodies
no one has ever loved. The shadow of death that
closes in illuminates these powers within oneself with
its black light. One knows there are things out there
that call for these powers.

Then, under the general and recurrent patterns of
the common world, one catches sight of visions offered to one's own eyes alone, appeals made to one's
own heart alone, tasks no one else sees, faces turned
to one's caresses and surfaces turned to one's laughter
and tears. They summon one, with an urgency that is
illuminated by the shadow of the abyss that constricts
one's heart. One will advance unto them, releasing
one's forces for them. In the forces that are one's

own, there is the force to die in the world on one's own.

But anxiety, which anticipates one's being cast into nothingness and stakes out the time of the possible, does not yet know the time in which one has to die. The death one anticipates in anxiety is both distant and imminent; it is the future moment, the fatal instant, that measures the paths and an array of tasks still ahead awaiting one's own forces. Anxiety quickens one's own powers to take hold of what is ahead. The death awaiting one is also imminent at any moment; in whatever one takes hold of, the abyss may take hold of one. But in whatever one takes hold of, one takes hold of a death that will be one's own.

The anxiety that anticipates one's death extends before one a time to act; the approach of death opens beneath one its own time. Between the death one takes hold of, and inflicts on oneself, when one takes hold of an implement to blow up the path ahead, between the drop of poison, the bullet, the thermonuclear warheads one unleashed on others and on all life on the planet, and the death that comes to take one, there extends the time it takes to die. Death comes, of itself; its approach is not locatable across the succession of moments each of which presents the possibility of the next one. When, in prostration, one feels it close at hand, one cannot take hold of what is there. Darkness, the unknown: it is not even apprehendable as the impossible, as nothingness. In action one extends the future, one retains a past behind one by gathering one's forces for possibilities ahead. Dying is to find oneself in a time that presents no possibility and that disconnects from one the past and its resources. One finds oneself held in a time disconnected from the time of a personal or interpersonal history, drifting.

Pain does not throw one back upon one's own resources; it backs one up against oneself; to suffer is to be unable to flee and unable to retreat from oneself. Pain senses the imminence of death. In the weight of one's own substance one can no longer bear, pain senses the weight of the unknowable that advances inwardly.

One suffers until the one that suffers is broken and shattered in gasps and sobs. One suffers as carnal flesh suffers, suffers with the suffering of all that lives and has to die. The others watch, suffering over one's suffering. One has to bear the pain, for them.

One can know the other as another one—parallel to, equivalent to, and interchangeable with oneself. One occupies a place another has vacated, and one will leave it for another to occupy. One seats oneself before tasks with movements picked up from others, passed on to others. One sees the inner diagram of posture in another, seated before a meal or opening a door to pull out a stretcher, and one views the meal as a meal one might choose to order or one reaches for the door for him. One sees others seeing things one could oneself see if one stood where they stand. One does not look at her but with her; following the path of her gaze, one divines the radius of things that attract her. When someone glances up from his tasks to one, one understands what he wants; when she extends her hand to one for help, one knows the move required.

To perceive him or her as different in the midst of this equivalence and interchangeability is to sense oneself bound to one's own place and tasks. One senses the wall of one's own death that separates the zone of possibilities that are possible for oneself from those that are for others. Another death circumscribes the expanse of possibilities that are possible for the other. The time of the world does not extend in a line where we each rejoin the evolution of the planet and the anonymous enterprises in the humanized map laid out on it. I come to exist in my own time, a trajectory extending back from the death awaiting singularly for me to my birth. I catch sight, about me, of other trajectories of time, disconnected from mine, in which others lay out a future for themselves this side of the deaths coming singularly for them.

Pain breaks down the path of time I am extending; I fall back from the future I was pursuing and the past whose resources I was drawing on, to sink into a time of enduring. In the pain I have a foreboding of the time of dying. The other suffers in another interval without equivalent and in a pain in which I can nowise displace him. Pain blisters in intervals of time coming from nowhere, going nowhere, disconnected from the past and future of life, of the transpersonal enterprises, of the evolution of the planet.

Yet it is out of that other time, the time of his or her dying, that the other addresses me.

To see the sensibility, susceptibility, vulnerability of another is to see not the inner diagrams but the substance of the body. It is to see the opaque skin, lassitude and torpor, into which the expressions form and vanish. It is to see the night of eyes, on which the forms of the world leave no trace. It is to see the spasms of pain that agitate the substance of flesh, the tremblings of pleasure that die away. It is to see wrinkles and wounds.

In pain the other sinks back into his or her body, into prostration that already delivers him or her to

death in the world. The flesh in pain is anything but
an object; sensibility, subjectivity fill it, with a terrible
evidence. This evidence is turned imperatively to me,
more pressing than the evolution of the planet and
the anonymous enterprises in the humanized map
laid out on it, more urgent than the tasks my own
death has addressed to me. It is not in elaborating a
common language and reason, in collaborating in
transpersonal enterprises, that the human community
takes form. It is in going to rejoin those who, fallen
from the time of personal and collective history, have
to go on when nothing is possible or promised.

She had been rolled back here on a cot from the lab-
oratory, from the three hours on a steel table where
electronic pulses scanned the inner organs hidden
within her and the doctor labored to insert the drain-
age, each probe of the steel needles sending seizures
of agony through the locally anesthetized organs and
glands. The puncturings and bleeding ravaged her
strength, her lungs gasped for air, her body was
drenched in sweat. They had wheeled her back into
the room, with the masks of efficiency and compe-
tence over their faces. They explained everything to
her, slowly and clearly, in quiet technical voices,
drawing diagrams and pictures, showing plates of
X-ray shadows. They explained, and left, for other
struggles, over the organs of others.

She lay now in the bed, immobile, her face gray
with exhaustion and drugs, her eyes opaque; it was
impossible to tell what she was thinking. She re-
sponded obediently to every question put to her, con-
centrating to answer correctly, then returned to a soli-
tude it was impossible to enter. They told her to try
to rest. Her worn and gnarled hands lay on the stiff

unwrinkled sheets. She had never known anything but labor. She had never gone anywhere save to work, from the first trip she took, as an indentured servant, from the hamlet in Eastern Europe to the city on the other side of the planet. Through the depression years, through the childbearing that had torn her entrails, through the five years she had, alone, cared for her bedridden husband, she had always done what she had to do. She had spent the past weeks meticulously going through all the tasks in which she was committed, terminating what had to be terminated. There was nothing more she could do in her garden and her kitchen; she sent the last of her canning to those she would no longer visit in the old folks' home. Her labor had already extended beyond death. She had set out to answer now for the effects and the continuation or the termination of her tasks by others after she was no longer there to carry them through. She found there was nothing more she could do for her children, who had abandoned her. Now her body was in the hands of technicians, no longer hers to mobilize and harden with resolve.

She did not rummage in her memories to relive them, to share them with others. It did not occur to her to make any statement, about the significance of her life, the significance of her death. She did not ask for any pledge, any commitment, from anyone. The nurse told her she could have her pain medication as often as she wanted it. The nurse attached the bulb with the medication into the IV and told her again she could increase the dose anytime she needed it. The nurse asked her if it had been strong enough last night. She did not seem to remember. She smiled and thanked the nurse. As though nothing she had learned or experienced could be drawn on now. She

did not complain, or ask for any help when she struggled to shift her body when the cramps came. It was
as though no one knew what she had to do, as
though those who knew were all infinitely out of
reach.

The doctors came and lied to you, lying, probably,
to themselves. They said the fluids they were injecting had the power to eliminate all pain. They said
they would monitor the dosage so that the effect
would be complete. They said she would sleep. They
said she would fall into a coma, and pass away in
rest. But as they spoke you heard the heaving of her
lungs, the convulsive gasping as of someone ship-
wrecked on icy seas; the gasping tore through your
chest and pulled at the windows, the doors, the walls.
You could hear nothing but the gasping.

Her organs were perforated, choked with bile and
blood, but the lungs and heart and muscles, strong
from so many years of labor, struggled to bear the
ragings of the torture in them. Her body struggled
with each stage of the decomposition, struggled each
time to establish equilibrium at another level, a ship-
wreck victim struggling to stay on the surface to pull
in air and then being hurled below again by another
surge of the limitless oceans in the night.

You seized the telephone and dialed Mexico,
where her friend had gone to recover in the home of
a doctor friend. Her gasping pulled at your ears; you
could not hear the sound of the ringing.

Finally someone said something, in Spanish you
could not make out; then it was her. You were afraid
of what your voice would do; you heard yourself giving a report of the doctors' report, a technical explanation you did not understand yourself. You said,
"She is so weak."

ACCOMPANIMENT

She just said, "I am coming."

You put down the phone, and bent over her and said, "She is coming. She is coming. She said, 'I am coming.'" Her eyes were open upon you, but there was no expression whatever on them. Her lips tightened in the straining to gulp in some air, formed no sign. Her hands were rough, the palms open and warm; her stiff fingers gave under the touch, opened. Her arms lay wasted by the labor of years, numb with the pain. Her face was gray, her cheeks lay loose over her, the warmth lay in them like in the springtime soil of her garden. Her broad, high forehead lay exposed and glowing with pale light. It was warm and damp. The hand that passed over it found nothing to knead or soften, no ridges tight or spasmodic, but movements like the stirring of minuscule organisms in the soil of her garden. Her eyes slowly closed under the hand laid softly over them.

She came at midnight, directly from the airport. She gave the cabby her address and asked him to leave her luggage at her home, and paid him. She came up to the room where her friend lay. She bent over her and kissed her over and over again on the face, on the hands, on the throat, on the chest, and called her name, very softly.

She opened her eyes and looked at her and smiled at her with a mouth that could not stop heaving and gasping for air.

She said she loved her. She said it again and again and then again. You knew she never hesitated to say that, immediately; she is entirely without defenses and without precaution. Those fearfully dangerous words.

She smiled as she gasped, smiled through the gaping openness of her mouth, smiled like a child smiles that has not yet discovered what cynicism there is in the world.

She smoothed the damp sheets, lifted the head from the pillow and smoothed the knotted hair, then lowered her head and lay her own head against hers. She said, "I will not leave you."

The nursing staff changed shifts; the doctors came in one after another in the course of the morning. But she refused to lay down to get some rest. She did go, by cab, to her house to clean up after the flight and to get some toilet articles. She returned in an hour. You had some lunch. She looked at you and thanked you for having telephoned. She thanked you again.

The other patient sharing the room was released in the afternoon; she left all her flowers for her. She lingered long with her, and rubbed her hand, stroked her face, and kissed her before she left. They did not bring another patient to the vacated bed. When the working day was over, her friends came, and stayed in the room, looking gravely at her, speaking softly to her just to tell her they had come.

She refused to lie down, but had coffee while they were there.

The night drifted into the room and closed in around the small bed lamp. It was deserted of everything save the heaving of her lungs, a harsh effort searing with pain that filled the room but never seemed to be able to swallow enough of a gulp of air before heaving again. No rumble of traffic from the street, no bustle from the corridor penetrated the room.

She worked to remove her dentures from the gasping mouth and then to swab the gums and tongue and throat of the thick mucus. It was very hard for her to replace the dentures in the mouth.

She herself raised her hand and tremblingly forced them into place. Then her hand fell back on the stiff sheets.

She grasped those jaundiced hands and moistened them with lotion, and caressed the hard creases and wrinkles. Hands she had clasped so many times, when they thought of something to do together, somewhere to go together. She clasped them firmly and clutched them to her bosom, and bent over her. She refused your entreaties to lie down on the adjacent bed, just for half an hour; you would be there, the whole time, you would make sure she would not drift off into sleep. She did not turn her grave eyes, her frail fingers, from the fever and the pain.

The nurses of the new shift came, checked thermometers, IVs, drainages. She had already bathed her, lifting the sheets and blanket corner by corner one after another, and had shampooed her hair, strand by strand, drying it, strand by strand, and carefully arranging it in the simple way she herself had done when she went out to her labors.

The doctors came in, one after another. The next shift of nurses came on the floor. The friends came in from work. She pulled each one up to the bed, insisted they speak louder, that she can hear, can understand everything. She understands everything, she insisted. They spoke, and withdrew to the corridor and cried.

She did not cry; not even a shudder of distress passed over her frail face, not once.

You pulled at her to step aside, to let them speak with her, to sit down and rest for awhile, you clutched her in your arms, but she struggled with a great violence in her body and pushed back into the room.

242

The blackness of the night invaded the room, cold
and infinite. The nurse brought in the vases of roses
the friends had sent. They gave off no perfume; they
drifted off, engulfed in the unending night.

The nurses left, the next shift came on, the doctors
came and looked at gauges and spoke of processes in
glands and tubes, and left. The friends came, and
spoke. She insisted that they speak, they speak in her
ears.

Her face suddenly twisted; she stopped gasping for
air and moaned and she bolted upright and thrashed
at the tubes in her arm, in her side, in her nostril.
The friends and she held her, they shook with the
torture within her, they absorbed it in their own
bodies, they contained it in their bodies.

She fell back on the bed and glared at them with
astonished eyes. The nurse rushed in with a needle
and said her name in a soft clear voice and said she
had to turn her on her left side. She immediately
tried to do it; she and the nurse supported her until
it was done.

She turned to the friends. "You see," she cried,
"she hears everything, she understands everything
perfectly. Speak to her," she cried. They said her
name, they said their names, they said they were
there, that they would not stop being there, even in
cars, even in offices, even in factories, they stood back
and wept. She would not allow herself to be per-
suaded or pulled away, she resisted saying she was
not tired at all, not at all.

Her skin was translucent, her eyes clear as the
spring skies, a smile floated continually on her. She
lifted the heavy body twisted with cramps and supported it on her frail limbs. She cleaned the soil and
laid a towel she had warmed on the radiator and

lowered her again, arranging the thin gray hairs around her head so that they drifted about on the pillow like the down of dandelions floating in her garden in early spring mists. She did not cease speaking her name, like an incantation, into the gray shells of her ears.

The rasping gulps in her throat pounded at the thick and surging night. Her face was radiant, her eyes opened wide, immobilized on her, her face was transfixed with awe.

VII

* * * * *

Chichicastenango

Copán, in Honduras, is celebrated by Mesoamericanists as the most beautiful of all the Maya ruins. Also
the most intact; the city and the river valley its people had cultivated had enigmatically been abandoned
four centuries before the conquistadors arrived. Four
centuries of tree roots had held and vines had hidden
its stones from the builders of colonial cities and
churches. In this century archaeologists from the
North came to clear away the jungle and expose
again its plazas, its temples, its great carved stelae.
U.S. ambassador John Stevens had personally acquired
the entire city in 1840 for fifty dollars. The first pri-
ority was to redirect the river, which had shifted the
direction of its force and had eroded the city's highest
part. Every summer teams of specialists work to map
out with helicopters and infrared scanning the roads
and buried ruins, to advance the excavation, to reas-
semble the walls overturned by the jungle, to dig up
burial grounds and measure bones and teeth and subject them to radiation scanning. When they leave
they continue to work over the data, in university
buildings filled with computers, to publish mono-
graphs—historians, sociologists, linguists, agronomists,
biologists. A multinational corporate industry, trans-
forming these ruins whose hewn shapes were effaced
by five centuries of bacteria, lichens, roots, and rain,
into texts. Texts filed in microchips, reinstated in the
great text of world civilization. Soon one will not

have to come here at all; one will tap numbers into one's home modem and these ruins will be restored as a city; one will watch its priests and nobles circulating in hologram in one's own living room.

I bought a bagful of the latest publications and went to have lunch in the village inn. The dining room was full of people; I had to wait long to be served. The others were finished as I began to eat; one of them stood up and began to give an account of the most recent findings by pathologists who had studied the data derived from the burial sites as to what these people fell ill of and died of. The others were taking notes, already busy on their future publications. Abruptly I recalled that Copán was the principal research site in Central America of the physical anthropology department of my own university. I could not focus my mind on what the professor was saying in the noonday heat. I did not introduce myself. I walked to the site with my bag of literature. I studied the great stelae, thick figures cut in high relief, not idealized human bodies as in the art of what we call classical antiquity; their torsos are studded with other figures, their limbs fitted between psychedelic protuberances, every inch of the space about and above them filled with enigmatic carvings. Soon I tired too of reading all the explanations before each marked site; I could do it this evening in my room. I gazed at the stelae much worn by the elements, craggy rocks recemented in the plazas now cleared and leveled, turned into parks. I strolled about the constructions which had sunken or whose upper layers had collapsed and had been reassembled; behind them the tangled jungle rustled with monkeys and birds. The once precision-cut stones no longer fitted together; sometimes cement had been needed to hold

them. High staircases led from level to level of the
city. One had to climb them in strictly designated
paths; there were signs warning of the instability of
either side. Wherever I looked I saw stones eroded,
cracked, their relief effaced, lichens and bacteria
gnawing at them. By the time the great text was
completed, the stones of the city would have sunken
into the planetary crust. The worshippers and the
gods had vanished from these ruined temples centuries ago. The campesinos who had recently cultivated
their patches of maize, *milpas*, in these ancient plazas
had been relocated elsewhere; now on the leveled
lawns young mestizo men of the village who had
been educated in English in government schools were
reciting the explanations the scientists had summa-
rized for them to the moneyed tourists. I became
weary in the heat and damp of the afternoon; I sat
down on a rock in the shade spread far by an enormous ceiba tree that had grown on the highest point
of the city walls, its massive trunk splayed at the bottom to send roots down in all directions seeking the
solid strata beneath, over which the city had been
built. I contemplated the multicolored lichens spreading like acidic stains over the stones. The vegetation
was dusty with tiny insects. I quickly gave up flailing
them off; their minute stings drew nourishment from
the torpor of my body. The wet humus and rotting
leaves rose to fill my breath. The theories—historical,
sociological, religious—were getting tangled in my
mind, which could not sustain interest in them. Even
images faded out. The ruins about me depopulated
even of their ghosts. The clear-toned calls of unseen
birds echoed in my skull. The slight swaying of the
trees and displacements of splatches of sunlight neu-
tralized into a dense medium without color and form.

I don't know how long I remained in this lethargy;
gradually I became aware not of eyes but of a look
before me. The look was mild and fraternal. Little by
little about the look a deer materialized, knee-deep in
the vegetation. It was a soft gray I had never seen on
deer, with white belly and tail. It was so close I
slowly shifted and reached out to touch it, but however I turned it always seemed to be the same distance from me. Little by little its gray turned to
smoke and then charcoal as night fell. When I finally
made my way to the entrance gate, it was locked; a
high fence with five strands of barbed wire on top
surrounded the site. I tore my clothes and cut my
hands and legs getting over it.

The received judgment is that the Maya civilization was the greatest of the Americas; its cities grand
as Harappa, Memphis and Thebes, Rome; its agriculture so sophisticated that the today unpopulated
marshlands of el Petén and the Chiapas rain forest
once supported vast populations; its science—the Mayas discovered the zero a thousand years before Europe; they calculated the Venus year to six seconds of
what today's electron telescopes have fixed as exact—
one of the greatest spiritual achievements of humanity. Where have they gone?

But fully 50 percent of the population of Guatemala today is pure Maya stock; one can see them on
market day in Chichicastenango.

Conquistador Pedro de Alvarado contracted with
one side, then another, of two rival Maya nations in
the high mountains of Guatemala, then betrayed them
both. The remnant of the smaller nation was put in strategic hamlets, *reducciones,* in the lowlands; that of
the larger group was resettled in the ruins of the
former capital of their rivals. The Aztecs conscripted

in Pedro de Alvarado's army called it Chichicastenango, "The Place of the Nettles." The conquistadors garrisoned there had mansions of stone built.
Franciscans arrived and set the Indians working to construct an enormous church rising over a great flight
of steps over the former Quiché sacred rock. The place
was remote; the only road descended in rocky switch-
backs down and then up a deep gorge.

I went to Chichicastenango. By the entrance of the
town there is a large billboard with the words *Dios
Familia Patria* and *El Ejército es su Amigo*—"God,
Family, Country" and "The Army is your Friend."
Campesinos are still arriving, bent under huge baskets
or heavy bundles of firewood. Many have walked the
whole night. They are very small, with parched
brown skin, the women dressed in extravagantly colored full skirts, the men in dust-clogged pants and
wearing straw hats with the brims smartly turned up
at the sides, down in front and back.

Chichicastenango has hardly grown in five centuries; from the central plaza one can see the whole
town, its streets stopped on all sides at the brink of
gorges but four blocks away. The plaza is filled with
stands. Down its narrow lanes blankets, hats, embroidered blouses and intricately woven skirts, iron picks
and shovels and machetes, painted masks, fruits and
vegetables, and salt are piled high. Tourists under
broad cloth hats, enervated by the altitude, the sun,
and the dust, are peering desultorily into the stands;
occasionally one of them decides, after some confused
bargaining, to buy something, and the others gather
protectively as she or he extracts some quetzales from
a moneybelt. Troops in combat dress carrying auto-
matic rifles walk through the streets with impassive
faces. In the center lanes of the plaza women are

cooking pans of beans and corn, vegetables, stir-frying chicken, while conversing in their melodious tongue. Laughing children chase one another around the stands. The men, alone or in groups, are getting drunk on *chicha*. One walks the lanes over the decaying husks of fruit, wrappings of leaves and twine, dirty plastic bags, broken bottles; in alleys and in doorways swept by the wind they pile up, splattered with urine and vomit, under swarming flies.

Some distance away there is an empty lot where women in bowler hats are gossiping, holding in their fists the cords tied tight to the rear legs of black pigs. Some of them have a half-dozen pigs on leash. The women turn away and hide their faces in their shawls if you lift your camera.

From the whitewashed tower of the church dedicated to Santo Tomás—Thomas the Doubter—the bells begin pealing. The church stands high in the sun over twenty feet of steps; the lower steps on one side are piled with bundles of gladiolus and calla lilies around women whose blouses under lace mantillas blaze with crimson, gold, and royal blue. Above them in the thick smoke of sacrifices smoldering on the steps, men are swinging incense burners. I hear the high-pitched repetitive melodies of flutes dancing over the beat of drums; the officiants of the Quiché communes are arriving, dressed in embroidered jackets and black knee-length pants with elaborate headdresses of plumes and animal fangs and carrying maces of burnished silver. The flower women make a path for them, and they climb the steps to the church entrance and disappear between men throwing dusty squalls of incense.

The main entrance is forbidden to those who do not know the secret Quiché formulas with which to

invoke ancestral spirits; I make my way to the cloister
on the right side of the church and enter through a
side door. The church nave is long and high and
filled with sticky perfumed smoke. Women are standing on the right side, men on the left; I cross over
and move halfway up to the sanctuary. Every ten feet
down the center aisle, there is a small raised cement
block upon which charred chickens and pieces of pigs
are smoldering in the midst of mandalas of flower
petals. Over them men in workclothes are swinging
incense burners. I realize that they are the spiritual
guides the Quiché call *chuchqajau*—"mother-father."

A white-haired priest enters from the sacristy to
begin the mass; the Quiché officiants are already
standing on both sides of the sanctuary with their
hands closed over their maces. A marimba band in
front of the altar rail begins to hammer out repetitive
cadences. Men and women are continually stepping
into the center aisle, placing on the fires packets
wrapped in leaves and consulting the crouched
chuchqajaus who stand up and make wide-open-
armed gesticulations in different directions before
receiving the next supplicant. When the priest has
reached the climax of the mass, the consecration of
the bread and wine, he lifts the host and chalice high
over his deeply bowed head; down the length of the
center aisle the chuchqajaus are occupied in making
different kinds of ritual dances over their consultants.
No one approaches the altar rail to take communion.

When the mass is over the priest disappears into
the sacristy; the Quiché officiants descend from the
sanctuary preceded by flutes and drums and leave
through the main portal. I see along the side walls of
the church only a few chapel altars; the carved statues
of saints, black with soot, have been crowded upon

them. On a few of these altars glass has been fitted over a painting, no doubt from the colonial epoch but barely discernible under the coat of grime. I look down the length of the now empty church; with its blackened walls and ceiling and the charred statues of saints pushed together against the walls, its sooty windows with many broken panes, it looks like an old warehouse abandoned after a fire.

On the side of the plaza I notice a piece of cardboard with the word *museo* and an arrow on it. I find two rooms with handmade cases of glass housing some broken precolumbian Quiché pots decorated with red pictures and designs, gold and jade pieces restrung into necklaces, incense burners, sullen deities congealed in brick-red clay. It turns out that this was the collection made by Padre Ildefonso Rossbach, whose faded photograph hangs in an aluminum frame on one wall. A sign says that he had been pastor of the Santo Tomás church from 1898 until his death in 1948. Campesinos had brought him these things they turned up with their plows, and he had told them not to sell them to the tourists. In the photograph Padre Rossbach looks German.

In Central America, the ruling families still send one son to the seminary; they preside over the great basilicas with altars encrusted with gold in Guatemala City, Antigua, Tegucigalpa, San Pedro Sula, Managua. But, save for a few old priests drinking and looking after their offspring in the mestizo and Indian towns, almost all the little churches in the mountains are untended and boarded up. Those that have mass celebrated and children baptized in them periodically are tended by missionaries. These have come from missionary orders in Portugal, Ireland, the United States.

Such idealistic young men have now too become
scarce. Those who came, and found themselves isolated for long months in dusty and famished villages,
often took up the Liberation Theology that was formulated originally in the favelas of Rio de Janeiro
and has since been silenced by the Roman Curia.
During the seventies and eighties, and in Guatemala
especially during the dictatorship of Rios Montt, they
were often the first to be massacred when the troops
arrived in the Indian highlands. Last year the priest
was killed in nearby San Andrés, a village on the
edge of Lake Atitlán much visited by tourists.

After eating some corn and beans in the plaza, I
descended into the gorge on the east side of the town,
crossed a small marsh and the in-this-season insignifi-
cant river, and looked into the forested hills that rose
at once on the other side. From one of them I could
make out a thin ribbon of smoke trailing into the
blazing sky. I walked through milpas of parched corn-
stalks, and found a path into the trees. The path rose
steeply and I trudged with slow steps like the old
campesinos and had to stop several times until my
heartbeat stabilized.

On top there was a circle of rough stones. Against
it, a flat black rock about three feet high upon which
one could see a face. It was roughly carved, one side much
narrower than the other, the eyes not on the same
level. They did not look at me, and the expression was
impassive. The stone had been broken across the face
and cemented back together. Up against it there was a
bundle of gladiolus, not in a container of water, wilted.
Within the circle of stones and outside it, there were several piles of greasy ashes, still smoldering, and limp
flower heads laid in lines and circles. All around the

256

dusty ground was littered with chicken feathers, all ragged, some spotted with black blood; the leaves under the trees were clotted with them.

I sat down under a tree at the edge of the clearing. There were many long-needled pines in the forest, and the wind hummed in their thin branches. There was no other sound; even the locusts were silent in the heat of the day. After awhile I looked back at the shrine. There was now an old woman with one eye opaque laying a packet wrapped in leaves on the embers, and moving in a kind of slow dance. Then she turned and vanished in the forest as silently as she had come.

The noonday sky bleached out the forest and forced shut my eyes. I heard the sludges of my body pushed with uncertain pulses. The essential is that sweat, secretions, vapors depart from it. The body's thrusts are expulsions. Its orifices expel urine and excrement, also phlegm, mucus, tears, groans. The feelings that irradiate in me are discharged down its nervous fibers. My brain crystallizes insights, thoughts, projects, destinies only to expel them from its gray mass. Everywhere humans move, we leave sweat, stains, urine, fecal matter. The organized constructions of our sentences flatten into bromides, erode into clichés, deteriorate into prattle, collapse into sighs, screams, sobbing, and laughter in orgasm. What we call construction and creation is the uprooting of living things, the massacre of millions of paradisal ecosystems, the mindless trampling of minute creatures whose hearts throb with life. We level mountains to pave them with temples whose gods become forgotten and with markets settling into rotting husks and plastic bags. The beat of our life is relentless drives to discharge our forces in things left behind;

our passions charged with revulsion and awe are excremental. Our blood shed, breast milk, menstrual
blood, vaginal discharges, and semen are what is sacred in us, surrounded from time immemorial with
taboos and proscriptions. Bodies festering, ruins crum-
bling into a past that cannot be reinstated, ideas and
ideals that are enshrined in a canon where they no
longer light the virgin fires of first insight in our
brains, extend the zone of the sacred across the mold-
ering hull of our planet.

Indians of Guatemala, driven to the high mountains by the ranchers who in the past twenty years
have deforested the hills below for the raising of
grass-fed cattle for hamburgers, Indians driven into
Chiapas in Mexico during forty years of army rule,
Indians dwarfed and stunted by chronic malnutrition.
Indians stumbling all night under the weight of their
handcraft, standing in lanes covered with debris and
rotting vegetables, when night comes leaving under
their heavy unsold bundles. Their Catholicism in disintegration, barely visible through the debris of
Quiché myths and rituals of a civilization destroyed
five centuries ago.

I was haunted all day by a sentiment I had felt
nowhere in my country in neogothic cathedrals
squeezed between high-rise buildings in cities or mod-
ernistic churches surrounded by spacious lawns and
parking lots in the suburbs. The sacred hovered in-
conceivably in the charred hull of the once Catholic
temple, in the broken idol in its circle of rough stones
on the hill outside the town, in the grime of sacrificial stones and torn and bloodied chicken feathers, in
the stunted bodies of Indians hunted down in these
rocky heights by soldiers from the capital transported
by helicopter. No, the sacred is this decomposition.

The sacred is what repels our advance. The taboos and proscriptions that demarcate it do not constitute its force of withdrawal. It is not the salvific but the inapprehendable, the unconceptualizable, the inassimilable, the irrecuperable.

One had to come this far, to this disheartening impasse of intellectual and conceptual activity. One had to come to this excretion of inassimilable elements. One had to come in a body breaking down in anguish, dejection, sobs, trances, laughter, spasms, and discharges of orgasm.

Religion advances triumphantly over the decomposition of the sacred. From its turbid ambiguity, religion separates the covenant from the taboos; the celestial order from the intoxication with spilt blood, milk, and semen; the sublime from the excremental. Its intelligence separates a celestial and divine order from the—demoniacal—world of decomposition. It levitates the sacred into an extracosmic empyrean, where a reign of intelligible providence and a paternal image of a personalized deity function to foster in humans exalted phantasms of undecomposable sufficiency. It consecrates the profanation of the world, given over to industry, information processing, tourists bused to the market of Indians while soldiers tread through the lanes with Uzis.

I got up and returned down the path and this time followed the river at the bottom of the gorge. Tangles of dirty plastic bags hissed in the scrub bushes. After awhile I came upon the gate of the cemetery, which lay above on a height facing the city from the west. At the entrance there are stone and cement family mausoleums in which the creoles are buried. Behind them graves with simple headstones. And then more and more graves without even crosses or names, with only mounds of clay to mark them. Here and there on the rocky ground there are black smudges of ashes, with circles of flower petals.

At the back of the cemetery there is a structure like a small chapel; it has been cracked as if by an earthquake, and most of the once yellow stucco has crumbled off its bricks.

Inside on the floor there is a large cross of raised cement: it is the grave of Padre Rossbach. Rays of light fall upon it from the half-collapsed roof. The floor is black with the tarlike grime of sacrificial fires, chicken feathers stuck to it or drifted into corners. There are wilted flower petals in lines and circles. The walls are completely caked with soot. In back two men and a woman are bent over candles and packets wrapped in leaves. Padre Rossbach has been transformed into a Quiché ancestor, revered with rituals centuries old when Christianity first arrived in this hemisphere.

I thought of his photograph. Germany was not sending Catholic missionaries to Central America; he must have been an American. I imagined a missionary order from a traditional rural area settled by Bavarians, in Wisconsin or South Dakota. He came here to take over the Santo Tomás church, in a small town of creole landowners and Chinese merchants and thousands of Indians come from the mountains on market day. He learned Quiché, discovered in the hamlets in the surrounding mountains their social order intact, the elected elders serving without salary, in fact having to expend all their resources to help in emergencies and to stage complex rituals. On market day they came to him with problems with the landowners and army. They brought offerings of corn and chickens, and sometimes old pottery they had had in their hamlets for generations. There was no money to paint the church, repair the altars. There were no nuns to run a school. The Cardinal Archbishop in Guatemala City did not visit outposts of foreign missionary orders. Little by little he let the Quiché people come in their own garb, which the Franciscans five centuries ago had forbidden, knowing that the apparently decorative patterns were so many woven amulets invoking Maya demons. He let the marimba players come in with their instruments, and when they began to play what were not hymns he did not stop them. He let them burn incense on the entrance steps, built over an ancient shrine. He himself took down altars which he was told were built over sacred stones. He ceased to demand that they consecrate their unions in matrimony. He ceased to demand that they come to tell him their sins in confessions. He let their officiants come with processions of flutes and drums into the sanctuary, the chuchqajaus to burn sacrifices in the center aisle. One day a delegation of *alcaldes*, village elders, showed him an ancient copy of the *Popoh Vul*, the great myth of the Quiché, which the world had believed lost irrevocably when Bishop Juan de Zumarranga in 1526 ordered all copies of the Maya sacred writings be burnt. They let him come to their meeting house night after night to copy it. He learned the sacred script, and was spending more time studying it and pondering its meaning than reading his breviary. The Quiché brought their children for baptism; it was the only one of the seven sacraments that were still performed in the Santo Tomás church. He must have opened his door to women who brought him chicha for the long cold nights, and received them in his bed. How many children called him padre? His last trip back to the motherhouse in the North American midwest was before the war; his parents were gone and his relatives dispersed, and he found he had difficulty expressing simple things in English. He returned to the chuchqajaus he knew, who came with remedies and spells during his last illness.

I thought of the afternoon of the first time I had come to Chichicastenango, eight years ago. I was sitting in the doorway of a building on the side of the plaza emptied by the sun, save for a few women who were tending pans of corn and beans over charcoal fires. A troop of soldiers crossed the square. The steps of the Santo Tomás church were smoking from multiple sacrifices. A boy brought me a glass of water, and did not stop to talk. Then I heard the heavy beat of a drum, and a single flute repeating a thin succession of tones. A procession of campesinos entered through a side street. I picked up my camera, but stopped cold. A peasant, perhaps thirty years of age, was stumbling behind them, under the dead weight of the body of a woman he was bearing on his back, her arms and legs limp across his steps. His wife. His grief bearing the weight of the dead— words that as they formed in my mind filled me with the shame of their hideous banality. The widowed peasant and his companions stopped at the steps of the Santo Tomás church and the chuchqajaus burnt fires and swung incense burners before the entrance to the ancestors who dwell in the great rock below. They did not enter the church and the priest did not come to accompany them and bless the mountain grave to which they advanced. Now I thought that the unembalmed corpse of Padre Rossbach too had been borne on the back of some Indian who had loved him and whose heavy steps had not carried him up the steps to the altar of the Santo Tomás church.

It was dark and cold now in the crypt. The campesinos had gone, leaving their smoldering fires. I was shaking, I did not know whether with sobs or with laughter.

The night had fallen and the town was dark with the mountain cold. The streets were empty; the campesinos were already dispersed in the mountains. Most of them must have sold nothing, I thought; they are bearing their now still heavier burdens back, to be packed up and carried again the next market day. The streets were ankle-deep in discarded husks and leaf-wrappings, dog and human excrement. Down every lane I was startled by the rustling of vaguely visible transparent forms. I told myself it was the wind whipping a snag of plastic bags, though each time I seemed to catch sight of a half-decomposed cadaver fleeing through the night in a luminous shroud.

In a week I must leave, and return to the state university where big classrooms will be full of students preparing, with textbooks and computers, their futures in the gleaming technopoles of the First World. They are identifying and assimilating information. Their appetite is young and healthy, like their appetites in supermarkets big as warehouses piled with a half-dozen kinds of apples, oranges, cheeses, prepared meats, fish, dozens of kinds of wine and liquors, unloaded from tractor trailers from remote states and ships and jet airplanes from remote continents. Like the appetite they bring to shopping malls piled up with clothing, furniture, stereophonic sound systems, television sets and VCRs, computers, motorcycles, automobiles. The appetite they will bring to resorts selling snowmobiles, marinas selling yachts, realestate agents selling condominiums and restaurant chains.

Everything abandoned in the onward advance or in death will be resold; everything outdated or worn out will be recycled. They are being trained by professors deciphering the genetic codes of living things, reducing the heterogeneity of snowflakes, gases and rocks, asteroids and galaxies to classified series of concepts, laws, formulas. The tabooed and the prohibited, the excremental and the marvelous will be conjured from the future; everything strange, departing, decomposing will be recuperated in the dragnets of knowledge. Their religion but one strand in the dragnets.

The working class created by the first industrial revolution is one that is deprived of the means to appropriate the materials and machinery of its labor. For them, industrial waste product, life does not consist in labor for the means to be freed of labor but for the means to lose themselves in the violent discharges of orgasm. The students I will return to will be agents in the third, information-processing, industrial revolution; they will not be workers.

The room was cold, there was nothing to do but take off my shoes and crawl under the blankets with my clothes on. I felt weary, and sleep, as for the old, came slow and fitful. From time to time I heard the slow steps of campesinos outside. Warmth finally came to fill my bed, the warmth of secretions and sweat, of ejaculations and stains.

I would have liked one of them to come to me with chicha and to be received into my bed. Someone with face wrinkled by the mountain sun and hands gnarled by labor.

Notes

Tenochtitlán

Tenochtitlán was written in Mexico City in 1988.

Photograph: Mummified child in the cemetery at Guanajuato.

1. Bernal Díaz del Castillo, translated as *The Discovery and Conquest of Mexico,* by J. M. Cohen (Middlesex: Penquin Books, 1963), 191.

2. Marcel Mauss, *The Gift, The Form and Reason for Exchange in Archaic Societies,* trans. W. D. Halls (London: Routledge, 1990).

3. Friedrich Nietzsche, *On the Genealogy of Morals,* trans. Walter Kaufmann and R. J. Hollingdale (New York: Vintage, 1989), 70.

4. Kenelm Burridge, *Someone, No One* (Princeton: Princeton University Press, 1979), 96.

5. Bartolomé de las Casas, *Apologetica Historia Summaria* (Mexico City: Instituto de Investigaciones Historicas, 1967), 183.

6. Díaz del Castillo, *The Discovery and Conquest of Mexico,* 407–408.

7. See Pierre Klossowski, *La monnaie vivante* (Paris: E. Losfeld, 1970).

8. Fernand Braudel, *Capitalism and Material Life 1400–1800,* trans. Miriam Kochan (London: Weidenfeld and Nicolson, 1973), 330–331.

9. Francisco López de Gómara, *Cortés, The Life of the Conqueror by His Secretary,* trans. Lesley Byrd Simpson (Berkeley and Los Angeles: University of California Press, 1965), 407–408.

10. Søren Kierkegaard, *Fear and Trembling,* trans. Walter Lowrie (Princeton: Princeton University Press, 1954), 49.

NOTES

A Doctor in Havana

A Doctor in Havana was written in Havana in 1991.

    1. Reported by Robert Cohen, United Nations Bureau Chief of the Nicaraguan News Agency. This passage is excerpted from a copyrighted article by Robert Cohen titled "In Brazil the Women Boast About Their Plastic Surgery." The article was published in the number 25, Winter 1986 issue of *Covert Action Information Bulletin* (now *Covert Action Quarterly*). Their address: 1500 Massachusetts Avenue, NW, Washington, D.C. 20005.

Tawantinsuyu

Tawantinsuyu was written in Qosqo, Peru in 1990.

    1. Marino Orlando Sánchez Macedo, *De las Sacerdotisas, Brujas y Advinas de Macho Picchu* (Lima: Empresa editora Contentel Peru S.A., 1989), 130.

    2. Anthropologist Alan Kolata, who worked for ten years on the Tiwanaku site in Bolivia, taught the local population the techniques of canals and raised fields developed by the Tiwanaku civilization by 1,000 B.C. They then grew seven times the amount of food they had been growing with modern techniques.

    3. David Cook Noble, *Demographic Collapse: Indian Peru, 1520–1620* (Cambridge: Cambridge University Press, 1981).

    4. Hiram Bingham, *Lost City of the Incas* (New York: Duell, Sloan and Pearce, 1962), 188.

    5. Qosqo legends of the imperial period tell that Manko Qhapaq was turned to stone, as also Ayar Kachi and Ayar Auka. Qosqo mythology tells of the conversion of the sons of the sun into stone, as also, conversely, stones converted into soldiers called *puruaukas* who defended the Incas when they were besieged (Sánchez Macedo, *De las Sacerdotisas, Brujas y Advinas de Machu Picchu*, 188).

Body Count was written in Manila in 1988.

Matagalpa was written in Matagalpa, Nicaragua in 1983.

NOTES

Antarctic Summer

Antarctic Summer was written in Antarctica in 1993.

1. White-out was the bane of the explorers; they and their dogs fell into crevices neither had been able to see.

2. The great white, tiger, and mako sharks feed on seals and sea lions, and sometimes mistake surfboard riders for them. They most often lose interest in a human victim after the initial bite. There have been only one hundred fatalities from shark bites in Australia during the past 150 years.

3. "No pain, no death is more terrible to a wild creature than its fear of man. A red-throated diver, sodden and obscene with oil, able to move only its head, will push itself out from the seawall with its bill if you reach down to it as it floats like a log in the tide. A poisoned crow, gaping and helplessly floundering in the grass, bright yellow foam bubbling from its throat, will dash itself up again and again on to the descending wall of air, if you try to catch it. A rabbit, inflated and foul with myxomatosis, just a twitching pulse beating in a bladder of bones and fur, will feel the vibration of your footstep and will look for you with bulging, sightless eyes. Then it will drag itself away into a bush, trembling with fear" (J. A. Baker, *The Peregrine* [Harmondsworth: Penguin, 1970], 100).

4. Diane Ackerman, *The Moon by Whale Light* (New York: Vintage, 1991), 133–134.

Lust

Lust was written in Bangkok in 1990.

1. Charles Baudelaire, *Oeuvres complètes,* ed. Claude Pichois (Paris: Gallimard, 1961), 1256.

2. Jacques Lacan, *Écrits,* trans. Alan Sheridan (New York: W. W. Norton, 1977), 72–77.

3. Gilles Deleuze and Félix Guattari, *Anti-Oedipus,* trans. Robert Hurley, Mark Seem, and Helen R. Lane (New York: Viking, 1977), 338.

4. J. G. Ballard, *Crash* (New York: Vintage, 1985).

5. Jean-François Lyotard, *Libidinal Economy,* trans. Iain Hamilton Grant (Bloomington: Indiana University Press, 1993).

6. Michel Tournier, *Friday,* trans. Norman Denny (New York: Pantheon, 1969), 192–194.

7. Gabriel Garcia Marquez, *In Evil Hour,* trans. Gregory Rabassa (New York: Harper & Row, 1979).

8. Shirley Lindenbaum, "Variations on a Sociosexual Theme in Melanesia," in Gilbert H. Herdt et al., *Ritualized Homosexuality in Melanesia* (Berkeley: University of California Press, 1984), 337–361.

9. Jean Baudrillard, *Seduction,* trans. Brian Singer (New York: St. Martin's Press, 1979), 96–97.

10. Daniel Wit, *Thailand—Another Vietnam?* (New York: Charles Scribner's Sons, 1968), 62.

After the Sambódromo

After the Sambódromo was written in Rio de Janeiro in 1993.

1. Adolf Portman, *Animal Forms and Patterns,* trans. Hella Czech (New York: Schocken, 1967).

2. David Grossman, *Voir ci-dessous: amour,* trans. Judith Misrahi and Ami Barak (Paris: Seuil, 1991).

3. Immanuel Kant, *Critique of Judgement,* trans. Werner S. Pluhar (Indianapolis: Hackett, 1987), 103–132.

Pura Dalem was written in Ubud, Bali in 1989.

Khlong Toei was written in Bodhgaya, India in 1982.

Coals of Fire was written in Dhaka, Bangladesh in 1982.

Accompaniment was written in Illinois in 1988.

Chichicastenango was written in Chichicastenango, Guatemala in 1993.

Designer:	ReVerb, Los Angeles
Compositor:	Braun-Brumfield, Inc.
Text:	11.5/13.5 Monotype Walbaum
Display:	Truth
Printer:	Edwards Bros.
Binder:	Edwards Bros.

DATE DUE